EAT Stop EAT

THE **SHOCKING TRUTH** THAT
MAKES WEIGHT LOSS
SIMPLE AGAIN

EAT *Stop* EAT

BRAD PILON

The information in this book is for educational purposes only. The information in this book is based on my own personal experiences and my own interpretation of available research. It is not medical advice and I am not a medical doctor.

The information within this book is meant for healthy adult individuals. You should consult with your physician to make sure it is appropriate for your individual circumstances. Keep in mind that nutritional needs vary from person to person, depending on age, sex, health status and total diet.

If you have any health issues or concerns please consult with your physician. Always consult your physician before beginning or making any changes in your diet or exercise program, for diagnosis and treatment of illness and injuries, and for advice regarding medications.

This book is dedicated to the loving
memory of Dr. H. Frank Farmer

More titles by Brad Pilon at
www.clkbooks.com

CONTENTS

A SPECIAL NOTE ON THIS EDITION

First of all, let me be clear that I was well aware of the immense gap between people's attitude toward health and fitness and the theories found within this book back when it when was first published in 2007.

I knew that people had generally accepted that strict dietary restraint and an almost relentless workout program were essential for weight loss. Not only this, but it was believed that a serious lifestyle modification had to occur that made you almost obsessed with health and nutrition.

I was all too aware that for some curious reason we had accepted the idea that losing weight had to be extremely difficult and the concept that long-term weight loss success meant a life of dedication and extreme discipline.

Back in 2007, even the slightest suggestion that we could actually cause a genuine reduction of body fat WITHOUT extremely regimented and inflexible dietary restrictions was often met not only with disbelief, but also hostility. Few were prepared to hear or accept a simpler solution.

The diet industry is huge, and worth billions of dollars in annual profits. This not only includes the obvious examples of over-the-counter diet pills, but also weight loss centers, weight loss coaches, weight loss books, and even online weight loss societies.

Combine this with the shocking boom of twenty-something-year-old internet marketers making millions selling "diet advice" online, and it becomes obvious that the weight loss industry was ready for a big, strong dose of common-sense thinking.

I knew that *Eat Stop Eat* was going to cause a shockwave in the diet industry, and that I was going to have to spend a great deal of my time defending the concepts within it..

But like I said, this was almost a given. It is the NORM for radical new concepts that receive a lot of attention to arouse a sharp division of opinion among expert "commentators."

Yet the fight for *Eat Stop Eat*'s acceptance was not nearly as uphill as I had imagined. Sure, it had its detractors and nay-sayers, but for the most part even the harshest scientific critic quickly came to realize the simplicity and effectiveness of *Eat Stop Eat* and appreciated that it was supported by very sound and logical scientific evidence.

It seems that in a matter of just a few short years, *Eat Stop Eat* has gone from being a controversial "fringe" dietary fad to becoming an accepted dietary approach to losing weight that is being supported by doctors, dietitians, and other mainstream health experts.

Biologist J.B.S. Haldane said it best when he pointed out that there are four stages of scientific acceptance:

1   This is worthless nonsense

2   This is an interesting but perverse point of view

3 This is true but quite unimportant

4 I always said so

Eat Stop Eat has hit the "I always said so" phase of acceptance. This is very exciting to me, and many others involved in the diet and weight loss industry.

People have begun to accept that losing weight can be accomplished using a multitude of different diets, as long as the diet creates some sort of decrease in caloric intake.

Not only this, but the concept that the best diet is the one you enjoy and can stay on the longest, has really caught on.

Despite these facts, there is still a growing amount of nutrition misinformation that is available in the mainstream weight loss industry. And, quite ironically, obesity rates are still increasing. In fact, the average percent body fat in North America has become startlingly high.

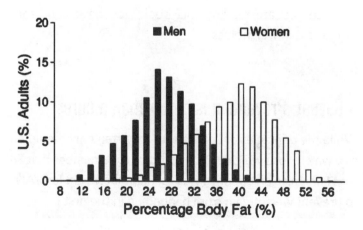

The average body fat percentage for men
is 25% and for women is closer to 40%.

Common sense and sensibility merges with the weight loss industry

The simple truth is that research illustrates an increased supply of food is more than sufficient to explain this obesity epidemic.[1] I am almost positive that no one is happy with the North American average of 25% and 40% body fat for men and women, respectively.[2] As such, there is still a need to expand on the successful theories of *Eat Stop Eat* to help as many people as possible realize that weight loss does not have to be complicated.

Let's start with what we already know about weight loss:

- Carrying extra body fat is really bad for us, both physically and emotionally.

- Weight loss is not a mystery and the fundamental principles have never changed. It's our ability to apply these principles that dictates how successful we are at losing weight.

- Since you are reading this book, you have a personal interest in weight loss.

A Caveat: Prevention is better than a cure

While the principles of *Eat Stop Eat* are often only thought of as a way to lose weight, it is important to remember that *Eat Stop Eat* is also an effective way to maintain weight loss, AND to prevent weight gain from happening in the first place.

Simply put, when adapted to fit your own personal lifestyle, the principles of *Eat Stop Eat* can apply to everyone.

PREFACE

Take a second before reading this book and think about all the diets you have heard about and read about in recent years. Each diet had its own little hook that made it stand out, and each diet had thousands of loyal followers who swore that their diet was the only one that worked.

Now consider the real-world evidence that is right before your eyes. Every day you see hundreds of people, all with different body shapes and all following different diets.

I will use professional bodybuilding as an example. Imagine two groups of bodybuilders ready to step on stage at the highest level of competition—their veins popping out everywhere with tanned, oiled skin and almost nonexistent body fat.

The first group consists of bodybuilders from the 1950s and 1960s. These bodybuilders were able to get into phenomenal shape using diets that were low in fat and high in carbohydrates with moderate amounts of protein. The second group consists of bodybuilders from the 1990s and beyond. They got into phenomenal shape using very different diets that consisted of moderate amounts of fat, low carbohydrates, and very high amounts of protein.

Both groups of bodybuilders were unbelievably lean. Both groups used various supplements and drugs. However, both groups followed very different nutrition plans. Yet, somehow they all managed to get their body fat down to unbelievably low levels.

Throughout the last five decades, the diets of bodybuilders have changed dramatically. Depending on the bodybuilder and the era, they may have eaten six meals a day or they may have eaten more than a dozen. Some bodybuilders ate red meat, while others did not. Some did hours of cardio and some did no cardio at all, yet they were all able to lose fat and get into "contest shape."

The reason all these bodybuilders could get in shape on so many different styles of diets is simple: for short periods of time, every diet will work if it recommends some form of caloric restriction. And if you follow a calorie-restricted diet, you will lose weight, guaranteed.

The problem is, you simply cannot follow a super-restrictive diet for a long period of time. Sure, a truly dedicated individual may be able to follow a very restrictive diet for 12 weeks and get into phenomenal shape. With the right amount of dedication, a person can even look like they just stepped off the cover of a fitness magazine. And a very small and unique group can do this for years on end.

For the rest of us, this way of eating is too restrictive, too intrusive on our lives, and far too limiting to be done effectively for any real length of time.

Now, what if I told you that these types of long restrictive diets are simply not necessary for weight loss? What if I told you that there is a way to eat and a way to live that can give you amazing health benefits, help you lose weight, and does not involve any prolonged periods of food restrictions, eating schedules, supplements, or meal plans?

On the following pages, I am going to share with you a discovery that I made as a result of years of research and schooling, a career in the sports supplement industry, and an obsession with nutrition.

I am going to present you with the reasons why I think most diet plans are unnecessary, too restrictive, and ultimately too complicated to work long term. And most importantly, I am going to describe what I believe to be the single best way to eat and live, which will help you lose weight and keep it off without any of the complex plans, rules, and equations that is typical of most diets.

After all, I don't consider this method of eating a diet. It's a way of eating that restricts calories, but can also ultimately grow into a way of life.

I must warn you in advance, many of these ideas are "different" in that they do not agree with the current nutrition trends. I promised myself when starting this project that I would not merely accept the current rules of nutrition just because they happened to be the rules that are currently *en vogue*.

As the bodybuilders in the example prove, many different styles of nutrition can result in the development of astonishing physiques. There probably is no "right" way to eat. The best we can hope for is finding the way that works the best for you.

Nutrition, just like all science and medicine, is always evolving and changing. So even though the ideas in this book may be unconventional by today's standards, I believe that someday they just might be the new rules of nutrition!

I am positive that if you read this book with an open mind, you will find that everything I have written makes sense. It may be different than what everyone else is telling you, but it is proven and backed up by a large quantity of scientific research, and it can change your life.

HOW IT ALL STARTED

I walked away from my career in the sports supplement industry in May of 2006. It wasn't a bad split, and I did not want to give up on the industry altogether, I just wanted to start fresh.

To fully explain this decision, I have to take you back about twenty years.

I have always been obsessed with exercise, health, and nutrition. At 10 years old, I could already boast a very impressive collection of *Muscle & Fitness Magazine*, and a couple of years later I was also collecting issues of *Men's Health*. I can remember reading about bodybuilders like Lee Haney, Arnold Schwarzenegger and Lou Ferrigno and all of the articles concerning their diet and exercise programs. It was these articles that piqued my interest in the science behind fat loss.

At 16 years old, I had a subscription to the *American Journal of Clinical Nutrition*. I would read any research paper that involved nutrition and fat loss. It would take me about a day to read each article because I had to stop and check almost every word in a medical dictionary.

At 17 years of age, I started working at a local supplement store. This was my first official step into the health and nutrition industry, and I have never looked back.

When I started studying nutrition at university, I had only two goals—to learn everything I possibly could about nutrition and metabolism, and to graduate with honors. In the spring of 2000, I accomplished both of them. Almost immediately after graduating from university, I was fortunate enough to be hired as a research analyst at one of the world's leading supplement companies.

Fast-forward to June of 2006. I had just spent the last six years of my life working in one of the most secretive industries in the world. During this time, I had been entrusted with protecting some of the most confidential information in the entire industry. I was the person responsible for the inner dealings of our Research & Development Department. Unfortunately, this was part of the problem.

Part of my job was to review bodybuilding and fitness magazines. Every month I would have to read through the top ten magazines on the market. I was constantly reading about the "latest and greatest" diet methods. After years of reading magazine after magazine, I didn't know what to believe anymore. Each month, it seemed like the newest diet methods contradicted the diet methods that were in last month's magazines. I started to think that the weight loss industry was full of nothing but confusing and constantly recycled misinformation.

When it came to the science of losing weight, every so-called "nutrition guru" and weight-loss personality had his or her own theories on what did and didn't work. After years of reading and evaluating all of these nutrition and diet programs, I was actually starting to ignore my previous doubts and get consumed by the hype!

Despite all of my formal education in the nutrition field, even the most absurd diet theories eventually started to sound logical to me, even though I had never come across any research that could convince me that these theories were supported by strong scientific evidence.

In reality, the vast majority of what I had read in these magazines was just theories and speculation. Some of them were based on science, while others were complete gibberish. Many were contradictory to one another, and others even defied the fundamental laws of thermodynamics and science.

Month after month, dozens of magazines would appear on my desk, and month after month, I would see new and old diet ideas being trumpeted as the newest, most effective way to "blowtorch through stubborn body fat."

At this point, I noticed a funny thing about the industry—if an idea is published enough times, and if enough people accept it, it becomes true, no matter how inaccurate it really is.

Whoever said, "You can repeat the same lie a thousand times, but it doesn't become any more true," has obviously never been involved in the nutrition industry!

The bottom line is that I got into the sports supplement industry for the same reason I eventually left. I wanted to understand the true rules of weight loss, and I wanted to figure out how we should really eat for health, energy, peak performance, and for weight loss.

I ended up leaving my career in the industry so that I could write this book.

INTRODUCTION

As part of the background research for this book, I made it my goal to uncover the true scientific facts behind weight loss and nutrition.

I'm not talking about the scientific "facts" that are thrown around every day by food companies and marketing gurus. You know, the "eat this, not that" facts or the "recent research has shown" facts. I wanted to find the cold, hard truths. I was looking for the nutritional equivalent of death and taxes.

My first step in this quest was to read every nutrition and diet book I could get my hands on. I read and re-read the following books:

> *The Atkins Revolution, Protein Power, Body for Life, The Zone, The South Beach Diet, French Women Don't Get Fat, The Warrior Diet, The Metabolic Diet, Volumetrics, The Obesity Myth, Health Food Junkies, An Apple a Day, What to Eat, the Omnivore's Dilemma, Real Foods, The End of Overeating, Eat Right 4 Your Type, Good Calories Bad Calories, Food Politics, as well as various underground books on diet and nutrition like Dan Duchaine's Body Opus.*

I didn't just read these books. I analyzed them. I compared marketing tactics, writing styles, and persuasion techniques. If the book quoted scientific references, I sought out the reference and reviewed it in its entirety. My goal was to dissect our current nutrition beliefs and to find their evolutions and origins.

On top of this, I also read and critically analyzed hundreds (not an exaggeration) of research papers, and re-read several of my nutrition textbooks.

I even went so far as to enroll in graduate school to study Human Biology and Nutritional Sciences, and let me tell you, it took an almost unhealthy desire to uncover the truth to drive me to re-enroll in school after a seven-year hiatus, with a pregnant wife and a busy consulting job! It was a long commute back and forth from school every day, but having the opportunity to study nutrition at the graduate level was worth the sacrifice.

So, what did all of my research uncover? Firstly, I can say that most (but not all) people who talk about scientific research online or in magazines are not credible sources of scientific information, nor can they properly analyze the meaning of any scientific research.

What they do is called "data mining," where they scan research papers looking for interesting sound bites or quotes. Basically, they try to summarize 2 to 3 years-worth of scientific investigation in one short and snappy quote. It's great reading, but it rarely gets to the truth of the topic. This is not meant as a self-serving ego-boosting statement, but rather as a testament to the importance of obtaining a proper education.

I also realized that even having an advanced education in one specific topic does not make you an expert in all things health related. Having a PhD in muscle physiology does not make you an expert in fat loss, and vice versa. Nor does being a medical doctor necessarily give you the scientific background you need in order to truly understand the complexities of nutrition, and more importantly to be able to see through the deceptiveness of nutrition marketing (many U.S. medical schools fail to meet the minimum 25 required hours of nutrition education set by the National Academy of Sciences).[3]

Finally, I can tell you that based on my research studying nutrition, fasting, and weight loss in graduate school, I have realized that there are only two absolute truths when it comes to nutrition and weight loss.

1 Prolonged caloric restriction is the only proven nutritional method of weight loss

   and

2 Human beings can only be in one of the following states: fed or fasted.

That's it. In my opinion, these are the only two facts that are undeniable. Everything else is open for debate, which is the problem with nutrition today—it is made out to be so complicated and confusing that nobody knows what to believe.

Most scientific research findings seem to do nothing more than add to the already confused and muddled nutritional theories and diet recommendations that exist, and the cause is clear as day—research on nutrition and food is no longer conducted to improve our health and well-being. It is conducted for marketing purposes and as a method to get us to buy one product over another, and it is all based on us being constant consumers.

In fact, it was in an amazing article in *Scientific American* magazine written by renowned food expert Dr. Marion Nestle where I became aware that it was in the early 1980s when food companies had no choice but to attempt to change the way we eat. Faced by stockholder demands for higher short-term returns on investments, food companies were forced to expand sales in a marketplace that already contained an excessive amount of calories.

Their only option was to seek new sales and marketing opportunities by encouraging formerly shunned eating practices such as frequent between-meal snacking, eating in bookstores, and promoting the money-saving value of larger serving sizes.[4]

To be clear, our entire style of eating in North America has been molded to support the interests of major food companies.

You may be wondering, "How can a select few people change the way entire countries decide to eat?" Well, in order to promote this new style of eating, enormous amounts of money had to be spent on research supporting the health benefits of this style of eating.

As far as I can tell, most research being conducted on food and nutrition these days is done simply for the purpose of food marketing. This is because the money that funds nutrition research is typically donated by a food company or supplement company.

This so-called "donation" or grant comes with the hope and expectation that the research will produce a health claim or other marketing claim that the company can then advertise as a selling feature for their product. As it turns out, health claims on foods and supplements can be incredibly lucrative, and the politics behind nutrition are undeniable.

It was in a book titled "*What to Eat*" by author and researcher Marion Nestle (the same author who wrote the article in *Scientific American*), where I read the following quote — "*The real reason for health claims is well established: health claims sell food products.*"[5] I couldn't agree more.

The bottom line is that research creates health claims, and health claims sell products. Whether the product is some new "functional" food or the latest diet program, if research says it works, it will sell more, guaranteed.

Very soon into my readings I began to realize that the research on weight loss had become so skewed with politics that it has turned into the world's most ironic oxymoron. After all, the research was trying to uncover the completely backwards idea — "*What should we eat to lose weight?!*"

When I realized that almost all nutrition research was working under this completely backwards paradigm, I understood that I had only one choice. If I was to avoid all of the bias and vested influence in today's nutrition research, then I had to go back to the absolute beginning. I had to conduct a thorough review of exactly what happens to human beings in the complete absence of food.

The Fasted State

The definition of fasting is quite simple. I've read through countless dictionary entries and website descriptions of fasting, and have decided that the best definition of fasting is the following: ***"The act of willingly abstaining from some or all food, and in some cases drink, for a pre-determined period of time."*** The key word in this definition is "willingly" as it is the difference between fasting and starving. Other than this one small difference, the net result is the same—the purposeful abstinence from caloric intake over a given period of time.

Now, a lot of people confuse "starvation" with wasting—wasting is the end result of prolonged caloric restriction where your fat reserves are almost completely used up and can no longer supply your body with enough energy to meet its needs. This is when you see abnormal physiology such as muscle wasting (loss), slowed metabolism and altered hormone profiles. So "wasting" is the end result of prolonged extreme calorie restriction—occurring after months or even years of a chronically low intake and possible nutrient deficiencies, but not something that happens in a 72-hour period without food.

So, you are either fed or fasted; however "fasted" can mean 12 hours or 12 weeks, so for the purpose of my research I decided to focus on short-term fasting, studying the metabolic effects of fasting between 12 and 72 hours. The minute you start fasting (stop eating) your body slowly begins to enter the fasted state. As you slowly use up the energy and nutrients supplied by your last meal, you also slowly begin to ramp up the amount of energy you supply from your body fat. For most people, you fully enter the fasted state using mostly body fat as a fuel, by about 24 hours since you finished your last meal.

So "fasting" begins the moment you stop eating, after which you slowly enter the "fasted state." The amount of time it takes to fully enter the fasted state depends largely on the size of your last meal, but in general occurs somewhere between 16 and 24 hours of fasting.

Throughout history, various cultures have used fasting in many different types of rituals and celebrations, and still use fasting within those traditions to this day. Almost all major religions have a degree of fasting built into them. From political protests to healing rituals, and even for good-old weight loss, there are many historical accounts of various people fasting for different reasons. With the exception of fasting for religious purposes, the practice of fasting has all but disappeared in North America.

Our ancestors also fasted simply due to the poor availability of food, or as a way to cleanse and heal their bodies. While modern-day humans in many developed countries are used to being able to eat a solid three meals per day, animals in the wild eat only when food is available and most likely this is also how our hunter-gatherer ancestors ate.

And let's not forget that the majority of the world's population still lives without adequate food supply. The fact that we're faced with a problem of too much food makes us the lucky ones. Of course, this creates an odd sort of irony in the fact that you are now reading a book about how to deal with the consequences of the extra food.

While researching, I observed that studying short-term fasting was an excellent way to uncover the truth behind nutrition and fat loss. This was because people with vested interests in selling consumable products have no interest in studying fasting.

Fasting automatically rules out the use of any sort of food, health supplement, or newly touted "functional foods." Much to the dismay of food companies, you can't put fasting into a pill and sell it; and as we have already discussed, the purpose of most nutrition research these days is the development of new products.

By default, because you do not consume anything while you are fasting, research on fasting contains very little bias from large food company funding. After all, why would a food company spend money proving there is a benefit to eating *less* of their products?

Another benefit of studying fasting is that there is an extremely large volume of research that has been conducted on fasting, and more research comes out almost every day. So, anyone who suggests there is no scientific data on fasting couldn't be further from the truth.

The Disappearance of the Fasted State

As I stated in the beginning of this book, from a nutritional point of view, a human being can only be fed or fasted. By saying this, I mean that we are either in the process of eating and storing the calories that come from our food, or burning these same calories as we burn stored energy. This energy is stored in the form of fat and glycogen (the storage form of sugars and carbohydrates in our bodies).

Our bodies are designed to eat food when food is available and use the calories we have stored as fat when food is scarce. These are our only two options. Consider them the yin and yang of nutrition and health.

FED — Eating and storing Calories

FASTED — Not eating and burning Calories.

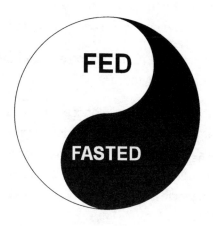

Fasting is the simplest method our body has for maintaining its caloric balance. Store a little when we eat, burn a little when we don't eat. Recent research suggests the problem is that we spend as much as 20 hours a day in the fed state.[6] We are constantly eating and storing food and we never really give ourselves a chance to burn it off.

So, the yin and yang of fed and fasted has been replaced by a constant fed state, where we helplessly try to figure out how to continue eating and somehow lose weight at the same time. This is a very scary scenario when you consider the fact that our bodies are designed to store fat whenever it is provided with an amount of calories beyond its needs. In order to restore the balance of fed and fasted states, we have no choice but to go through periods of undereating to match our large periods of overeating.

As a very crude example, imagine a hunter who has caught and eaten an animal, and foraged around and found some berries. Once the meat is gone and the berries have all been picked, the hunter has no choice but to move on in search of more food. Based on this ancestry, it seems logical to say that this is precisely how our bodies were designed to function.

So, if our bodies were designed to feed and then fast, why doesn't anyone fast anymore?

Most likely it is because the concept of fasting for weight loss and health has been villainized in western society as it goes directly against one of the most basic principles of business—supply and demand. To the food industry and various government agencies, the idea of people eating less is bad for business.

Consider that each day in the United States, the food industry produces enough food to supply every single person with almost 4,000 calories.[7] On top of that, 10 billion U.S. dollars per year goes into the advertising and promotion of this food.[8] It would be a huge financial disaster for many food companies if, all at once, everyone in the United States decided not to eat for one day out of the week.

This is why the food and nutrition industry is willing to suggest many different theories on how to lose weight, as long as it means we continue buying and consuming foods. And not only that, they're trying to sell the idea of buying MORE foods and consuming it MORE often.

Think of all the diet suggestions you know. They all rely on the continued intake of food. *Eat six small meals a day. Eat high protein. Eat breakfast (the TV commercials say it's the most important meal of the day). Eat cereal. Overeat. Cycle your carbohydrates, cycle your proteins. Eat lots of high calcium foods. Eat whole wheat. Take diet pills.* Whatever the recommendation, it always revolves around making sure that the population is continuously consuming food and food supplements.

After all, this is how companies refer to us—we are consumers (not people). And if you look up the word "consumer" in the thesaurus you will find that its synonym is "customer." How many times have you heard a company representative say things like, "We value our customer"? Well, of course they do! We buy (and consume) their products! Without us, there would be no profits and no company.

In a day and age where so many people are trying-and-failing to lose weight, it seems improbable that the answer is simply dieting. In fact, in his very controversial book *The Obesity Myth*, author Paul Campos states he does not believe that dieting is an effective method of weight loss. Indeed, Mr. Campos goes so far as to say the idea that, "People could lose weight if they really wanted to," is, in fact, a lie.[9]

Although I'm not willing to go quite as far as Mr. Campos, I am willing to say that every single one of today's popular diets is doomed to fail in the long term. In my opinion, no matter how strong your willpower, it will eventually be over-ridden by the power of marketing, advertising, and the lure of great tasting food. After all, no one really wants to diet, we just want to look better with less fat on our bodies. (Dieting just happens to be a rather uncomfortable means to this end.)

All of this raises the question: have we been led to overlook the simplest form of reducing calories and losing weight—short periods of fasting—in an effort to keep us consuming? The answer seems to be a resounding, "Yes!"

Forget Everything You Have Ever Read about Fasting

The amount of fasting misinformation that can be found on the internet is astounding. This is despite the fact that our bodies were designed to fast, that almost every major religion and culture has some sort of fasting built into its rituals to this day, and that most scientific studies that require blood collection also require their subjects to be fasted.

Information on fasting and dieting is prevalent in cyberspace and in popular diet books. However, this information should be read with extreme caution. Ridiculous statements such as: *"Fasting will KILL your metabolism,"* *"Fasting deprives your body of nutrients and does nothing to help you modify your dietary habits,"* *"The weight loss from fasting comes entirely from muscle,"* or *"The weight loss from fasting comes entirely from water,"* and finally, *"If you do not eat every 5 hours your liver releases sugar, which causes an insulin surge making you gain fat even without food,"* are typical of the fasting misinformation that is available.

This is an example of "authoritative parroting" (where people simply repeat what they have had heard from authorities on the topic, without actually stopping to check and see if what they have heard is correct). So, the same misinformation is passed on, regurgitated, repeated, and made true; solely on the basis of the source, rather than whether or not it is actually correct.

Other incorrect, but often repeated, statements include the notion that you will become hypoglycemic (have low blood sugar) if you do not eat every two to three hours and that fasting will prevent your muscles from growing. Typically, these statements are followed by more of the same old nutrition mantra, *"Eat multiple small meals a day," "Eat high protein foods every two to three hours," "Avoid milk and dairy products,"* and all the other popular ideas about dieting.

The amazing thing is almost all of the scientific research I reviewed provided evidence in direct opposition to the misinformation found in diet books and on the internet. I found very convincing evidence that supports the use of short-term (as brief as 24 hours) fasting as an effective weight loss tool.

This included research on the effects that fasting has on your memory and cognitive abilities, your metabolism and muscle, the effect that fasting has on exercise and exercise performance, and research that very conclusively exposes the myth of hypoglycemia while fasting.

What made this even more interesting is that this type of fasting not only helps you lose weight, but also vastly improves many markers of health and comes with a very impressive track record. After all, outside (and inside) of North America, millions of people have been using intermittent fasting for centuries.

As cutting edge as it may seem, taking brief breaks from eating is hardly anything new. It's just something that a lot of people have been trying very hard to keep you from realizing!

In fact, many people stumble onto fasting when they very first attempt to lose weight, and they usually see some success. They only give up on fasting after being convinced that it is bad and wrong by anti-fasting propaganda.

From a marketing standpoint fasting is boring. It does not have a sexy marketing angle and it certainly does not do anything to improve the bottom-lines of food companies. In this day and age, a diet has to have a hook or a catch. It needs something to make it different and special, and this typically involves some special way of eating, but never a special way of NOT eating.

Here is the common sense reason why fasting may work better for you than any other diet you have ever tried. Think of all the diet rules you have seen lately. It might be something that says you need to eat your carbs separately from your fats, or that you need to eat zero carbohydrates all together. Maybe it's that you need to eat all fat or that you need to cycle your carbohydrates or your protein. Perhaps it's the idea that you must only eat raw foods or organic foods, or it's a diet planned around a hormone like ghrelin, adiponectin, leptin, estrogen or testosterone... etcetera and etcetera.

Now consider this: If these rules were ACTUALLY true, then lap band surgery would not work. But it does, and it works very well.[10, 11]

During lap band surgery, a small silicon band is placed around the top portion of a person's stomach, effectively making your stomach "smaller." It's a very drastic step that involves a surgical operation, but nonetheless, it is extremely effective at helping people lose weight simply because it makes people eat less. Not just less carbs or less fat, but less everything. No periodic refeeds. No cycling. No crazy food combining. They simply eat less.

The bottom line is that a diet really does NOT need a catch to be effective. In fact, I would argue that the less compli-cated a diet is, the better its chances of helping you obtain long lasting weight loss.

The specific type of fasting I am about to describe is not just a tool for weight loss, but rather could be considered a fairly simple (yet effective) lifestyle adjustment that can help you lose weight and improve your health WITHOUT having to resort to special "rules of eating," taking pills or powders, or electing for invasive surgery.

Fasting and Your Metabolism

In my review of fasting, I found some very interesting information, most of which contradict much of today's accepted "rules of nutrition." Most startling is the fact that being in a fasted state for short periods of time will not decrease your metabolism.

If you have followed any of today's popular diets, you may know that they are all based on idea. The story they are telling goes like this: *if you lower r calories too much, even for a short period of time, then yo ill stop losing fat because your body has entered "starvatic ode" and your metabolic rate will slow to a standstill.* In fac is statement could very well be the basis for today's wei loss industry. However, it turns out that it is factually incorrect.

Our metabolism, or more corre y our metabolic rate, is based on the energetic costs c keeping the cells in our bodies alive. For example, let's s re put you in a fancy lab and measured the amount of calories you burned in one day sitting on a couch doing nothing. Let's assume that number was 2,000 calories. This would be called your basal metabolic rate; 2,000 calories would be the amount of calories you need to eat to match the amount you burn simply being you.

Now, let's say you moved around that day, perhaps 30 minutes of walking. You might burn an extra 100 calories bringing your daily total number of calories burned up to 2,100. Your basal metabolic rate is always 2,000, and then any extra energy you expend moving your body (such as when we exercise) is added to that number.

So in this example, you are going to burn 2,000 calories per day no matter what you do. So why are we being told that our metabolism will slow down if we do not eat for an extended period of time?

The answer lies with an interesting metabolic process of eating called *"the thermic effect of food,"* and some clever interpretation of this rather simple process.

The act of eating can increase your metabolic rate by a very small amount, and this is what is referred to as "the thermic effect of food." This increase in metabolic rate is a result of the extra energy your body uses to digest and process the food.

It takes energy to break down, digest, absorb, and store the food once you eat it. This "energy cost" has been measured in laboratory settings and is part of the basis for popular diets that promote the metabolic cost of one nutrient over another.

For example, it takes more calories to digest protein than to digest carbohydrates or fats, so some diets recommend substituting some protein for carbohydrates and fat assuming this will burn more calories. Although this is scientifically true, the amount of extra calories this dietary change will cause you to burn is very small and will hardly make a difference to your overall calories burned in any given day.

As an example, the idea of eating an extra 25 grams of protein so you can burn more calories can appear somewhat ridiculous. If you eat an additional 25 grams of protein, you would be adding 100 calories to your diet just so you can burn 10 more calories! The more logical approach would be to just not eat those 100 calories.

Almost all of the calories you burn in a day result from your basal or resting metabolic rate (the calories it takes just to be alive). Beyond that, the only significant way to increase the amount of calories you burn in a day is to exercise and move around.

The research on metabolic rate and calorie intake is remarkably conclusive. I was easily able to find the following research studies that measured metabolic rate in people that were either fasting, or on very low-calorie diets.

In a study conducted at the University of Nottingham (Nottingham, England), researchers found that when they made 29 men and women fast for 3 days, their metabolic rate did not change.[12] This is 72 hours without food. So much for needing to eat every 3 hours!

In another study performed at the Pennington Biomedical Research Center, men and women who fasted every other day for a period of 22 days experienced no decrease in their resting metabolic rate.[13]

In addition, a study published in 1999 found that people who were on very low-calorie diets and on a resistance exercise program (i.e. lifting weights) did not see a decrease in resting metabolic rate, and these people were only eating 800 Calories a day for 12 weeks![14]

In another interesting study published in the aptly-named journal "Obesity Research," women who ate half the amount of food that they normally eat for 3 days saw no change in their metabolism, either.[15]

In still more studies, performed on men and women between the ages of 25 and 65, there was no change in the metabolic rate of people who skipped breakfast, or people who ate 2 meals a day compared to 7 meals per day.[16, 17]

In a study published in 2007, 10 lean men fasted for 72 hours straight. At the end of their fast their energy expenditure was measured and found to be unchanged from the measurements that were taken at the beginning of the study.[18] Yet another example showing that fasting does not decrease or slow one's metabolism.

The bottom line is that food has very little to do with your metabolism. In fact, your metabolism is much more closely tied to your bodyweight than anything else. And, your metabolism is almost exclusively tied to your lean body mass or "LBM." This means all the parts of your body that are not body fat.

The more lean mass you have, the higher your metabolism, and vice versa. It doesn't matter if you are dieting, dieting and exercising or even following a VERY low-calorie diet. As the graph below illustrates, it is your lean body mass that determines your metabolism.

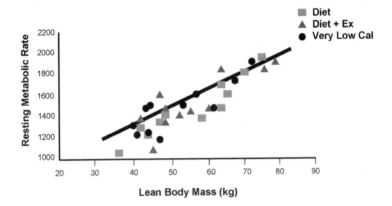

The only other thing that can affect your metabolism (in both the short term and long term) is exercise or movement. Even in the complete absence of food for 3 days, your metabolism remains unchanged.

I find it troubling that every physiologist, medical doctor, and PhD that I have talked to seems to understand this, but many of the personal trainers, nutrition personalities, and supplement sales people are completely unaware of this scientific fact.

This is truly a testament to the amazing power and persuasive nature of the marketing that can be found on the internet and in fitness and nutrition magazines. It is also an illustration of the scientific illiteracy of many of the fitness personalities and marketers you may deal with in your life.

This got me thinking that if short-term changes in food intake have no effect on metabolic rate, what other myths have I been led to believe as *scientific facts*?

I took it upon myself to examine the science behind many of today's popular diets. I found no difference between any of them in their effectiveness over the long term.

People choosing higher protein, lower carbohydrate diets (similar to Atkins or The Zone) tended to see slightly better weight loss, at least in the short term. However, when these studies extended to more than six months and up to a year, the differences tended to even out.[19]

I found only one thing to be consistent with all of these diets. This common finding is the success of any diet can be measured by how closely people can follow the rules of the diet and how long they can maintain caloric restriction.

In other words, a diet's success can be measured by how well they can enforce my first nutrition "truth"—**prolonged caloric restriction is the only proven *nutritional* method of weight loss**.

If the diet plan allows you to stay on the diet for a long period of time, then you have a very good chance of achieving sustained weight-loss success.

From what we have seen, there is a large amount of science that supports the use of short-term fasting as an excellent way to create a dietary restriction, and it seems to be an effective and simple way to lose body fat (which is ideally the goal of ANY weight loss program). On top of that, we have also determined that short-term fasting does not have a negative effect on your metabolism.

So far, so good. Fasting does not cause any negative or damaging effects on our metabolisms, but that still leaves us with another big unanswered question: what type of effect does short periods of fasting have on our muscles?

Fasting and Exercise

Your muscle cells have the ability to store sugar in a modified form called glycogen. The interesting thing about this process is that your muscles lack the ability to pass this stored sugar back into the bloodstream. In other words, once a muscle has stored up some glycogen, it can only be burned by that muscle and cannot be sent off for use by other parts of your body.

For example, the glycogen stored in your right leg muscles can only be used by your right leg muscles. It cannot be donated to your liver, brain, or any other part of your body. This basic rule goes for all of your muscles. This is in contrast to how your liver works. Your liver stores glycogen specifically for the purpose of feeding your organs, brain, and other muscles as needed.

During a period of fasting, the systems of your body are relying on fat and the sugar that is stored in your liver for energy. Your muscles still have their own sugar that they need for exercising. The sugar in your muscles is used up quickly during high intensity exercises like weight training and sprinting, but even a few consecutive days of fasting in the absence of exercise has little effect on muscle glycogen content.[20] By doing so, your muscle glycogen is truly reserved for the energy needs of exercise.

Generally, research has found that any effect that brief periods of fasting has on exercise performance is small. Research completed in 1987 found that a 3.5-day fast caused minimal impairments in physical performance measures such as isometric strength, anaerobic capacity or aerobic endurance.[21]

In plain English, they found that a 3-day fast had no negative effects on how strongly your muscles can contract, your ability to do short-term high intensity exercises, or your ability to exercise at moderate intensity for a long duration.

More research published in 2007 found that performing 90 minutes of aerobic activity after an 18-hour fast was not associated with any decrease in performance or metabolic activity.[22] What makes this study even more interesting is not only was fasting being compared to the performance of people who had recently eaten, but it was also being compared against the performance of people who were supplementing with carbohydrates during their workouts!

This means fasting does not negatively affect anaerobic short-burst exercise such as lifting weights, nor does it have a negative effect on typical "cardio" training.

Another study published in the *Journal of Applied Physiology* in 1988 found no change in measures of physical performance when soldiers were exercised until exhaustion either right after a meal or after fasting for 3.5 days.[23]

From this research, we can see that you should be able to work out while fasted and not see any change in your performance.

The only situation where I think there may be a negative effect from fasting is during prolonged endurance sports, like marathons or Ironman-style triathlons, where you are exercising continuously for several hours at a time.[24, 25] These types of ultra-long competitions typically require the athletes to eat during the actual event in order to maintain performance over such prolonged time periods.

In most research trials examining the effects of fasting on prolonged endurance activities it was found that fasting negatively affected both overall endurance and perceived exertion.[26] Keep in mind, however, that many of these studies were performed at the END of a 24-hour fast.[27] So it is not advisable to partake in a 3.5-hour bike right at the end of a 24-hour fast, but I'm hoping you already knew that.

It should be noted that the "negative effect" that occurs from fasting before a long endurance activity only affects an athlete's time until exhaustion (performance duration). So, the amount of time an athlete can exercise while fasted before becoming exhausted is less than the amount of time it takes for a fed athlete to become exhausted.

Even though fasting may decrease the amount of time it takes for an athlete to become exhausted, fasting actually has other positive effects, one of them being fat burning.

Athletes performing long endurance activities while fasted actually burn more body fat than athletes who are fed (because the fed athletes are burning through food energy before they get to the stored energy in their body fat). So depending on your goals, fasting before endurance exercise may actually be beneficial (so much for the idea that you absolutely need to eat a small meal before working out—this completely depends on your exercise goals).

Outside of these performance-based issues, I see no reason why you cannot exercise while you are fasting. The obvious anecdotal issue would be concerns about exercise during fasting being able to cause low blood sugar levels. However, this has been addressed in research conducted on experienced long distance runners.

In a study published in 1986, 9 men who were experienced long distance runners were asked to run at 70-75% of their VO2 Max for 90 minutes (this is a pace and distance that most recreational, gym-going people could never achieve). They completed this run twice. Once while in the fed state, and a second time a couple of weeks later when they were at the end of a 23-hour fast.

Surprisingly, when the blood glucose levels of the runner's first run and second run were compared, they found no difference between blood glucose levels during the two 90-minute runs. Not only this, but the fasting run also resulted in higher rates of fat burning.

It also took almost 30 minutes of exercise in the fed-state before the runner's insulin levels finally fell to the same levels that they had BEFORE they even started their run when they were in the fasted state.[28] In other words, after 23 hours of fasting, the runner's insulin levels had dropped down to the same levels you would have after 30 minutes of intense running. From a health point of view, that's a pretty amazing head start!

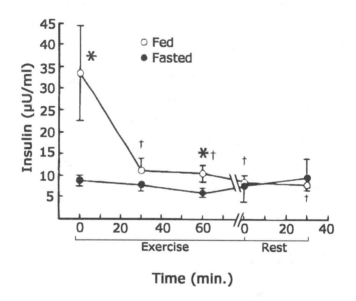

Time (min.)

Here is another interesting benefit of exercise while fasting. There are metabolic pathways that actually help maintain your blood glucose and glycogen levels while you are fasting, and exercise has a positive effect on these pathways.

During high-intensity exercise your muscles produce a bi-product called *lactate* (sometimes referred to as lactic acid). Lactate has been wrongfully accused of causing the pain in your muscles when you work out, and something called delayed onset muscle soreness—the pain you feel days after your workout. While lactate doesn't cause pain, it does help maintain your blood glucose and glycogen levels while you fast.

When lactate levels build up in your muscles as the result of exercise it can leave the muscle and travel to the liver where through a process called gluconeogenesis (making new glucose) it is associated with recovery of glycogen stores. So, exercise can help maintain blood glucose levels and glycogen stores while a person is fasting.[29]

In fact, it's not only lactate that helps to maintain your blood glucose and glycogen levels while you fast. The very act of burning fat also releases something called *glycerol* from your body fat stores. The free fatty acids in your fat stores are attached to glycerol while it is stored in your body fat. When the fatty acids are released, so is the glycerol.

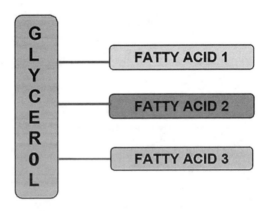

Three fatty acids attached to a glycerol "back bone."

Glycerol is a valuable precursor for gluconeogenesis in the liver. So, the very act of burning fat can also help maintain blood glucose and liver glycogen stores. And, since low intensity exercise tends to increase the rate of fat release and the amount of fat being burned as a fuel, you could say that both high-intensity and low-intensity exercise actually help to make your fasts easier by helping to regulate your blood sugar levels, and supply building blocks to help maintain your glycogen levels.

I believe the perceived need to eat before a workout or a strenuous activity is more of a psychological need than it is a physical need. Fasting has little to no effect on most forms of exercise, and exercising while fasting may actually make your fast feel easier by helping to maintain blood glucose levels and glycogen stores.

However, fasting is not advised preceding long-length endurance events, nor during the training of elite athletes if the training involves multiple workouts each day and where performance is the number one priority over body composition. But for everyone else the combination of fasting and exercise may be a potent way to lose body fat and maintain muscle mass.

Fasting and Your Brain

I think this myth may not be the fault of the nutrition industry as much as it is a carryover from our childhood. The idea that we must eat to fuel our brains may in fact be true for children, as research seems to suggest that children do better in basic school tests after they have had breakfast as opposed to when they skip breakfast.[30] This makes sense, as children are still growing and developing, but is it true for adults too?

As it turns out, the research doesn't really support the idea that you get "dumb" or "slow" when you haven't eaten for a couple of hours.

In a test where 21 university aged people were asked to perform a series of intellectual tests after having either a normal meal, skipping 1 meal, skipping 2 meals, or going 24 hours without food, researchers found no difference in performance on measures of reaction time, recall, or focused attention time.[31] This led the authors of the study to conclude that short-term food deprivation did not significantly impair cognitive function.

These results have been confirmed in additional studies where healthy young adults ate as little as 300 calories over a 2-day period and experienced no decrease in tests of cognitive performance (including vigilance, reaction time, learning, memory, and reasoning), activity, sleep, and mood.[32]

The interesting part was that in earlier research the exact same group of scientists found that when people were dieting for prolonged periods of time, they found the exact opposite results. They discovered that prolonged dieting did cause a slight decrease in cognitive function.[33]

So, while long-term self-deprivation may result in a lower ability to concentrate, it seems that short-term fasting doesn't have this effect. This leads researchers to suggest that the effect of long-term dieting on cognition may be more psychological than it is physiological.

Basically, when you are dieting for a prolonged period of time you perform worse because you tend to be grumpy and miserable or because you are unsatisfied with your body.[34] Whatever the reason, the research illustrates that short-term fasting, especially the method described in this book, doesn't produce this effect.

Not only has research shown that short-term fasting doesn't impair cognitive function, but it also suggests that long-term calorie restriction may improve memory in older populations.

When researchers put a group of 50 women with an average age 60.5 on a calorie-reduced diet for 3 months they found that the women had significantly improved scores on verbal memory tests.[35] So not only does fasting not impair your memory function, it may even improve your memory in the long run. And, as we discuss in later chapters, new research on fasting is currently uncovering a brain-protecting mechanism that is turned on by fasting (see the chapter on Cellular Cleansing).

Yet another myth about fasting has proven false.

Fasting and Your Muscle Mass

The other great myth about dieting and fasting is that you will lose your muscle mass while you diet. Based on the available research, this is completely false.

Preserving muscle mass seems to be a very important thing in the diet industry right now and for good reason. Muscle makes up a large proportion of your lean body weight, and for this reason muscle is a large contributor to the amount of calories you burn in a day.

While the idea that muscle burns massive amount of calories is a bit of stretch (every pound of muscle on your body only burns about 5 calories per day, not 50 like commonly stated), the fact that you can build or lose muscle makes the metabolic contribution of muscle very important. Not only that, you cannot deny the effect that muscle has on your body image. Being lean AND having muscle definition typically makes people feel good about themselves.

Luckily, not only does reducing your caloric intake not cause your metabolism to slow down, it also does not result in a loss of your hard-earned muscle.

There is one imperative rule that goes along with this statement. **You have to be involved in some sort of resistance exercise, such as lifting weights**. Now, to be clear, you do not have to weight train at the exact same time you are fasting, but resistance training must be occurring at some point for your muscle mass to be preserved in the face of a caloric deficit.

While long-term caloric restriction on its own can cause you to lose muscle mass (such is the case with hospital patients who are on a low-calorie diet and confined to bed rest), the combination of caloric restriction with resistance exercises has been proven to be very effective at preserving your muscle mass.

Research published in 1999 found that when men and women followed a 12-week diet consisting of only 800 calories and around 80 grams of protein per day, they were able to maintain their muscle mass as long as they were exercising with weights 3 times per week.[36]

In another study published in 1999, obese men restricted their caloric intake by eating 1,000 calories less per day than they normally ate for 16 weeks. They took part in a weight-training program 3 days per week and were able to maintain all of their muscle mass while losing over 20 pounds of body fat![37]

In yet another study, 38 obese women undertaking a reduced-calorie diet for 16 weeks were also able to maintain their muscle mass by training with weights 3 times per week.[38]

As long as you are using your muscles, they will not waste away during short periods of dieting. From my experience in the sports supplement industry, I can tell you that drug-free bodybuilders and fitness athletes constantly undergo 16 to 20-week periods of very low-calorie diets while maintaining all of their muscle mass as they prepare for bodybuilding contests.

The muscle preserving effects of exercise are even evident in older populations. When 29 men and women between the ages of 60 and 75 dieted for 4 months, the group that was exercising experienced no significant decrease in lean mass, while the group that was not exercising had more than a 4% decrease in lean body mass.[39]

Even more good news comes from the fact that your weight workouts don't have to be painfully long to be effective. When 44 overweight women performed a 30-minute weight training workout 3 days per week for 20 weeks while following a low-calorie diet, they were able to lose almost 5% body fat while maintaining all of their lean body mass.[40]

Finally, research has clearly shown that fasting for as long as 72 hours (regardless of whether or not you are exercising) does not cause an increased breakdown in your muscle, nor does it slow down muscle protein synthesis.[41, 42]

Another diet myth busted!

Fasting and low-calorie diets DO NOT cause you to lose muscle mass if you are resistance training. In fact, as we will discuss in the "Fasting and Inflammation" chapter, fasting may actually decrease some metabolic factors that are actually preventing you from building muscle. And, as we will discuss the "Cellular Cleansing" chapter, fasting may perform critical maintenance and "clean up" work in your muscle that properly prepares it for extra growth. So in the long-term, fasting and weight loss may actually improve your ability to build muscle mass!

So much for the so-called starvation mode or needing to eat protein every couple of hours—the key to maintaining your muscle mass long-term is resistance exercise; your diet has almost nothing to do with it!

And since your diet has very little to do with your muscle mass, then short periods of fasting definitely will not cause your muscles any harm (especially if you continue to work out regularly) and may even help you build muscle in the long term.

A Note on Fasting and Increasing Muscle Size

While the research is very clear that fasting for 24 hours will not cause you to lose muscle, it does not address the issue of whether or not fasting can impede muscle growth.

The process of muscle growth is still a vague collection of physiological phenomena that is not completely understood. What we do know is that muscles respond to certain types of mechanical stress by being damaged, repairing themselves, and under the right circumstances, increasing in size and capacity to generate force.[43] This process involves a whole cascade of events including, but not limited to: a local inflammation response, the activation of satellite cells, satellite cell incorporation into damaged muscle cells, the movement of amino acids into the muscle cells, then finally growth. And all of these events seem to be orchestrated through the influence of multiple hormones and signaling molecules, including testosterone, growth hormone, myostatin, mTOR, and possibly even insulin.

There seem to be two basic nutritional requirements to ensure all these processes lead to muscle growth:

1   Caloric Adequacy

2   Protein Adequacy

You'll notice that the first point is caloric *adequacy* and not caloric *surplus*. While the common belief is that you need to "eat big to get big," recent research has shown that any extra calories consumed above your estimated daily needs do not contribute to muscle gain. In fact, almost every single extra calorie can be accounted for in fat mass gains.[44]

So, while there is an obvious caloric need for muscle building, it does not seem to be any higher than your daily calorie needs (building muscle does take energy, but it also happens very slowly). Plus, if these calories are going towards the energy needs of building muscle, they cannot, by definition, be a surplus. Another way of looking at it is that if they were stored as fat, they couldn't possibly have been used to build muscle.

This is where *Eat Stop Eat* may actually be BETTER than traditional dieting for muscle gains. With *Eat Stop Eat* you are only in a calorie deficit for one or two 24-hour periods per week. The rest of the time you can eat to maintenance if you choose to. This is in direct contrast to traditional dieting where you may spend months in a constant calorie deficit.

While the speed of muscle growth is very slow, the unique ability to have periods of calorie restriction and calorie adequacy do supply a sound theory as to why intermittent fasting may be a superior choice for people looking to build muscle while losing body fat. Especially since there is a small but interesting amount of evidence to suggest that fasting can actually prime the metabolic machinery to be more sensitive to the anabolic effects that protein intake[45, 46] and exercise[47] have on muscle growth.

While protein intake is also a hotly debated topic, I have found through my review of the existing research that intakes above the current recommended daily intakes does seem to aid in muscle growth and that any protein containing meals consumed within 24–48 hours following a resistance exercise session will contribute to muscle growth.[48]

Also, new research suggests that muscle growth may respond better to intermittent pulses of protein rather than a continuous supply.[49] It is speculative, but intriguing, to suggest that a 24-hour break once in a while may even be able to aid in the muscle building process.

It is well known that eating protein can increase muscle protein synthesis by more than two-fold; however, keep in mind that in almost all of the research studies examining how eating protein affects muscle growth, the protein was fed after a period of fasting. So, to describe the current body of research on protein and muscle growth accurately, it can be stated, *"After a short period of fasting, consuming protein can increase rates of muscle protein synthesis for several hours."* In other words, you simply cannot ignore the fasting component of this research. This is not to say that after a fast is the only time eating protein increases protein synthesis, but it surely is one of the most studied times.

There has also been a considerable scientific research conducted to determine the optimal timing of protein intake in order to maximize the muscle building effects of a workout. In general, it seems to be largely irrelevant whether protein is consumed before, during, or after-exercise.[50, 51] And, even during the post-exercise period there seems to be very little difference whether protein is consumed immediately or several hours after a workout.[52] This is because anabolic effects of a resistance-training workout appear to last at least 24 hours.[53] This is why *protein sufficiency* rather than a specific *timing of protein intake* seems to be most important nutritional component of muscle growth.

To summarize, periods of caloric adequacy combined with an adequate protein intake and the proper stimulus seem to be enough to allow for muscle growth. And utilizing the occasional brief period of fasting combined with extended periods of eating at maintenance may actually allow for better muscle growth than long-term continuous caloric restriction. Finally, even if you want to consume protein immediately after your workouts it should be completely possible to organize 2-4 workouts in a manner that each of them could be followed by a post-workout meal while still allowing you to fast for 24 hours once or twice a week. In other words, as long as fasting and workout plans are organized properly, an occasional fast should not interfere with your ability to recover and support muscle growth after a workout.

A Final Thought on Fasting and Muscle Mass

While long-term caloric restriction on its own can cause you to lose muscle mass, the combination of caloric restriction with resistance exercises has been proven to be very effective at preserving your muscle mass.

As long as you are consistently using your muscles in a progressive and challenging manner, they will not waste away during short periods of dieting. Further, muscle mass can be preserved during longer periods of calorie restriction, so long as resistance training is part of the overall weight loss approach. Finally, intermittent fasting may provide a novel and unique method of increasing muscle size while at the same time reducing body fat.

2006   2009   2013

The above pictures are of me in 2006 while working in the supplement industry, (29 years old, 170 pounds); in 2009 after 3 years of following *Eat Stop Eat* (32 years old, 176 pounds); and lastly in 2012 after 6 years of following *Eat Stop Eat* (35 years old, 173 pounds). Hopefully you'll agree that I have not suffered massive muscle loss and may have even built some more muscle after 6 years of following *Eat Stop Eat*.

Fasting and Hunger

The true feeling of real hunger is difficult to explain and I'm not sure many of us have ever really experienced it. We have felt the withdrawal of not being able to eat when we wanted to, and the disappointment of not being able to eat what we wanted to, but true hunger is reserved for those who have gone weeks without eating and are not sure when or where their next meal will come from.

Consider that most people get noticeably hungry or irritated if they have gone more than two to three hours without eating. But during this time, metabolically speaking, they are still in the fed state. This means their bodies are still processing the food they ate at their last meal. There is still unused energy from their last meal in their system, yet they are already feeling hungry enough to eat again. How can this be?

Most likely, what we call hunger is really a learned reaction to a combination of metabolic, social, and environmental cues to eat. Remember how I mentioned that the food industry spends 10 billion U.S. dollars per year advertising food? Well, it turns out that this advertising is very effective.

According to Brian Wansink, author of *"Mindless Eating"* and dozens of scientific publications on why people eat, we make as many as 200 food related decisions every day and are subjected to countless food advertisements.[54] In my opinion, this is why almost all diets fail. It is virtually impossible for us to always be consciously in control of what we eat and how much we eat. There are just too many environmental factors (like advertising and fast food availability) that are working against us!

The role of taste and smell in motivating a person to eat (and in the food they select to eat) is fairly obvious. Perhaps less obvious is the role of habit, social influence, and cephalic reflexes.

For the most part, I believe that hunger as you and I understand it is a conditioned response created through the mix of tastes, smells, habits, and social influence. In other words, our desire to eat is determined by a combination of our body's response to the amount of food we have eaten, and our mind's response to all of the environmental factors around us (such as TV commercials and snack food packaging colors, fonts, and graphics.)

While it is easy to suggest that "hunger" and "cravings" are purely learned phenomena developed from infancy until we are adults, others argue that hunger is actually more of a biochemical phenomenon.

It has been argued that our constant desire to eat may even be related to a form of addiction. In the best-selling diet book, "*The South Beach Diet*," author Dr. Arthur Agatston refers to our love of sugar as our "sugar addiction."[55] He may have been on to something with that statement.

According to a recent article in *Scientific American Mind*, by psychiatrist Oliver Grimm, recent research suggests that drug addiction and binge eating are very similar in "neurobiological terms."[56] Put more simply, the brain reacts to food (not just sugar) the same way it would react to a hardcore narcotic like cocaine.

In another article from *Scientific American*, Nora D. Volkow, the Director of the National Institute of Drug Abuse, stated that food and illicit drugs both excite areas of the brain that are involved with reward and pleasure. Therefore, food can create a conditioned response that is evoked by the mere sight of food, or even by being in an environment in which these foods are consumed.[57]

While explaining food cravings and hunger in this purely biologically manner is intriguing—especially the connection between the psychoactive compounds in food and hunger— these concepts seem to be based more on speculation than substantial research findings.[58]

In reality, the total body of research seems to suggest that there are both biological and learned influences on appetite and that these two influences are highly intertwined and probably cannot be separated.

Evidence from a wide variety of sources supports the idea that eating motivation is not regulated according to a simple cycle of "depletion and repletion," but rather a series of motivational effects of the presence of food, its taste, smell, palatability, and a whole host of other external cues.

Within the last decade, it has been recognized that an increasing proportion of human food consumption is driven by pleasure, known as "hedonic hunger."[59] And this hedonic hunger creates many of our learned eating habits.

In other words, it is the way that we eat each day that teaches our body when to expect food, and even what kinds of foods to expect.

The exact term for this phenomenon is "food entrainment." In animal studies, we refer to the reaction to food expectation as "food anticipatory activity." And this isn't just a psychological thing (it's not just all in your head).

Food anticipatory activity includes increased locomotor activity, body temperature, corticosterone secretions, gastrointestinal motility, insulin secretion, and activity of digestive enzymes.[60, 61, 62, 63] So we truly can "teach" our bodies when and where to be hungry.

And, because much of hunger is learned phenomena developed from infancy to adulthood, the desire to eat specific foods in particular contexts (celebration) or in relation to particular feelings (stress foods) or situations (beer while watching football) can be regarded as a feature of normal appetite, rather than being an indication of some sort of eating pathology like an addiction or dependence. It is simply "how we learned to eat."

In fact, it is mostly social factors that teach us which of these learned hungers are right or wrong.

The desire to eat eggs at breakfast time and the desire to eat chocolate when relaxing and watching television in the evening may both be examples of specific learned appetites. However, only one of these learned appetites would be viewed as an addiction or craving.

In this sense, eating things you don't want to eat or that don't move you towards your goal is nothing more than bad habit that has been learned and ingrained through years and years of practice.

From my own personal experience with fasting, I can tell you that you do get used to the feeling of not eating, and not worrying when you will be eating your next meal. It becomes easier to manage as your body gets used to the feeling of having a truly empty stomach.

I am not certain if this is because you switch from fed to fasted at a quicker rate, or if it is just getting used to having an empty stomach, or if you are "unlearning" your typical eating habits.

Another possibility is that by learning the truth about fasting you get rid of the guilt you used to get when you thought you were doing something unhealthy by not eating every couple of hours. Whatever the case may be, it does get easier. Even when you do feel hungry while fasting, the hunger sensations usually don't last more than a few minutes.

Friends of mine who have adopted periods of fasting into their lives have reported a sense of freedom during the day, mostly because they do not have to spend time worrying about what and when to eat or the emotional stress of choosing appropriate foods. There is a definite feeling of being free from many of our previously held hunger cues, and this allows us to develop a much clearer understanding of what it takes to identify and control the reasons why we eat.

Often times, periods of fasting have been associated with being more alert, ambitious, competitive, and creative. Not only that, but you are no longer having to continuously plan your day around the timing of your next meal, and you may be "resetting" your body's expectation of when and how much you are going to eat.

Essentially, taking short breaks from eating allows you the opportunity to retrain your food anticipatory activity to allow you to eat less even on the days when you are not fasting.

Lastly, people are also often concerned that fasting will "make them hungry." Luckily, this concern can be addressed by research that studied the calorie intake of people after a 36-hour fast.

This research found that a 36-hour fast does not cause you to rebound and eat significantly more calories once the fast has been broken. Fasting for 36 hours tends to lead to a slightly larger breakfast the next day, possibly causing a 400-calorie increase for the day.[64]

This may sound extreme, but keep in mind the 36-hour fast caused an average of 2,800 calories worth of deficit, so even with 400 extra calories at breakfast the next day, there was still a total deficit of 2,400 calories. If you like the glass half full perspective — a 36-hour fast created a 2,400-calorie deficit AND allowed for an extra big breakfast the next day!

The bottom line is that fasting allows people to unlearn some eating habits, or at the very least become aware of some of the key cues that cause them to overeat, and short-periods of fasting do not induce a powerful or uncontrolled need to compensate on the subsequent day by vastly overeating.

Fasting and Blood Sugar Levels

I'm guessing that at some point in your life you have heard someone say they are "hypoglycemic" or that they have "low blood sugar." Typically, this is used as part of the reason why this person needs to eat every couple of hours to keep their "blood sugar stable."

The basic story is that if they don't eat every 3 or 4 hours then they become hypoglycemic and become irritable, moody, light-headed, and shaky.

I find this an interesting phenomenon considering as little as 5-10% of the population actually have a malfunction in their ability to regulate their blood sugar levels. Also, there is no actual clinical consensus regarding the cut-off values for blood glucose levels that truly define hypoglycemia for all people and purposes.

It's important to note that I am not suggesting that hypo-glycemia does not exist. I am merely suggesting that the average person without an underlying medical condition does not have to worry about getting "low blood sugar" while they are fasting.

From reviewing the research, it is evident that unless you have drug-treated diabetes, hypoglycemia just isn't that prevalent in healthy people. This is because your body is amazingly effective at regulating the amount of sugar that is flowing around in your blood.[65]

Throughout the typical 24-hour cycles of eating, digestion, and fasting, the amount of glucose in your blood is generally maintained within a range of 70-140 mg/dL (3.9-7.8 mmol/L) as long as you are healthy.

To give you an idea of how truly remarkable this feat is, consider the following: The average human being has about 5 liters of blood. Looking at the numbers above and doing some quick conversions we realize that during any given day, the amount of sugar in your blood ranges from between 5 grams and 7 grams. This is roughly the amount of sugar in 1 to 1.5 teaspoons!

Research conducted upon healthy adults shows that mental efficiency declines slightly (but measurably) as blood glucose falls below about 65 mg/dL (3.6 mmol/L), or into the range of about half of a teaspoon.

It is important to note that the precise level of glucose considered low enough to be defined as hypoglycemia is dependent on the age of the person, the health of the person, the measurement method, and the presence or absence of negative symptoms.

According to the research I reviewed on the effects of short-term fasting on blood sugar, a 24-hour fast should not place you into a hypoglycemic state,[66] and I have not seen any research that has shown a subject going below 3.6 mmol/L blood sugar during a short-term fast.

So if there isn't any clinical evidence of short-term fasting causing hypoglycemia, what's with all these people who say they get moody and light headed if they don't eat every three hours?

In a paper titled *"Effect of fasting on young adults who have symptoms of hypoglycemia in the absence of frequent meals"* researchers aimed to answer this exact question.

Specifically, the researchers were interested in the glucose metabolism of subjects who had a history of what they considered to be hypoglycemic episodes (becoming irritable or feeling shaky in the absence of food).

8 people who reported a history of hypoglycemic episodes were compared to 8 people who have never experienced any form of hypoglycemia. Both groups completed a 24-hour fast while their blood sugar levels were monitored.[67]

During the study, none of the subjects in either group had any periods of documented hypoglycemia. In fact, after closer investigation it was apparent that when the group that had a history of "hypoglycemia" reported periods of "feeling hypoglycemic" while their blood sugar levels were at normal levels.

Both groups had a decrease in insulin and an increase in body fat being used as a fuel during the 24-hour fast.

The researchers concluded that there is no doubt that some people may find eating less to be more stressful than others, but as long as no other metabolic disease is present, the ability to maintain blood glucose in the normal range does not seem to be effected during a 24-hour fast.

They then speculated that the symptoms of hypoglycemia could in fact be related to anxiety and stress over not eating, as opposed to being caused by low blood sugar.

This anxiety could be over fear of becoming hypoglycemic, fear that they are doing something unhealthy by not eating, or even a drug-like withdrawal response to not being able to eat when they wanted to.

For whatever reason these feelings occur, the research seems very clear that while some people find eating less a little more stressful than others, short-term fasting will not cause you to become hypoglycemic.[1]

---

[1] Keep in mind that *Eat Stop Eat* is written for people without any underlying medical conditions. If you have diabetes or any other condition, please consult with your doctor.

Other Misconceptions of Fasting

There were many other misconceptions about fasting that I found while reviewing books, magazines, and websites. Of course, I also found through studying the metabolic effects of fasting that without a single exception every one of these turned out to be misunderstood research, incorrect information, or just poor journalism.

A great example of some of these misconceptions would be the effect that short periods of fasting has on the hormones leptin, testosterone, and cortisol, as well as the concern over missing breakfast.

Fasting and Leptin

Leptin is a very interesting hormone. It gets lots of buzz in the weight loss industry, mostly because of its effects in animal research. In 1994, researchers discovered that a specific strain of genetically modified obese mice had a deficiency of a certain protein-hormone called leptin, which is released from fat cells and is monitored by the brain.

Whereas normal mice had a gene that causes fat cells to secrete leptin, these mutated obese mice lacked this gene. When these obese and leptin-deficient mice were injected with leptin, their weight slowly returned to non-obese levels.[68] Shortly after this discovery, it was found that leptin could even increase metabolic rate (energy expenditure) in mice.

Thus was born the idea that differing levels of the hormone called leptin was the way the body regulated its fat levels, and the common belief that it controlled both appetite and metabolic rate.

The weight loss industry quickly jumped on this story, and leptin was hailed as the cure for obesity. When I began my research, I found the belief that *"changing levels of leptin were of vital importance to a person's fat loss efforts"* to be a troubling one, mainly because leptin has been shown to be very responsive to acute changes in human physiology. Anything from a decreased amount of sleep to 2-day periods of high intensity exercise and even short-term fasting are all known to dramatically reduce leptin levels for a brief period of time, and they do so without affecting a person's metabolic rate.

As it turns out, what works in mice, doesn't always work in humans. It has since been found that when leptin levels are reduced by as much as 80% in humans for a short period of time there is no change in their resting metabolic rates.[69]

In other words, short-term changes in leptin levels do not seem to have any influence on, nor are they influenced by, changes in resting metabolic rate in humans.[70, 71] However, this lack of connection between leptin and metabolic rate in humans in no way means that leptin is not important to human physiology or your fast loss efforts; in fact, nothing could be further from the truth.[72]

In humans, the leptin levels in our blood do seem to be correlated to the amount of food we eat. The more food we eat, the more leptin can be found in our bloodstream. Overeating for several days can increase leptin levels; however, these levels return to normal within several hours after the overeating has ceased.[73]

Leptin also seems to be correlated to the amount of body fat we have. The more fat we have stored, the more leptin tends to be circulating in our bloodstream.[74]

These facts lead us to speculate that leptin is some sort of monitor or signal for both the energy available in our energy stores and the energy that is being made available through the food we eat. Yet, leptin is even more complicated than this.

In humans, leptin also rises and falls acutely in different situations, and these situations are often counter-intuitive to the idea that leptin is intimately tied to the amount of body fat you have or how much food you have been eating.

As an example, both long-term endurance exercise and resistance exercise can cause reductions in leptin levels, as can fasting,[66] increased testosterone levels, and increased catecholamine levels. Even injected anabolic steroids can decrease leptin levels.[75]

In all these situations, leptin levels drop very quickly, too quickly to be a marker of the amount of body fat you have. In fact, in all these examples there is an increase in fat burning, despite massive drops in leptin levels, suggesting that acute changes in leptin levels may not be indicative of acute changes in fat burning. However, it does not disprove the notion that long-term chronic elevations or suppressions in overall leptin levels may have a direct influence on your ability to lose body fat.

Obviously, there is more to the leptin story than we know to date. Simply put, leptin isn't just a fat-sensing hormone. Short-term changes in leptin seem to have little to do with the amount of body fat you have or your ability to burn body fat, whereas long term, more chronic changes in leptin seem to be related to overall energy availability.

Leptin becomes even more complicated when we look into the research currently being conducted on leptin's role in regulating reproduction, maturation, and even its role in inflammation—specifically its pro-inflammatory role in chronic systemic inflammation.[76]

It has also been identified as playing a role in cognitive function, immune response, and even the ability to taste the sweetness levels in our foods and drinks.[77]

The bottom line is that leptin is an extremely important hormone that is intricately connected to the amount of fat you have on your body. It is also tied to appetite regulation and may even be involved in the fat burning process, however short-term fluctuations in leptin levels do not seem to be nearly as important as longer-term changes.

Drastically suppressed leptin levels are often found in elite athletes and have been associated with periods of over-training and long-term excessive calorie restriction, whereas chronically elevated leptin levels are associated with a proposed leptin-resistance that occurs with obesity, blunting leptin's ability to regulate appetite.

Leptin truly is a master hormone within our bodies, and one that is not simply a "fat loss hormone." For leptin, as with all hormones, the right amount isn't the highest amount, instead it is the amount that is optimal for your body. We do not want leptin levels driven high by obesity, and we do not want it driven too low by excessive long-term overuse of exercise and calorie restriction.

And, while short-term fasting typically involves an acute dip in leptin levels, the consistent increase in growth hormone (GH) ensures that fat loss remains elevated during periods of fasting (more on this in the next chapter). Plus, what happens acutely during a fast may not represent what happens in the long-term as a result of fasting.

In trying to ascertain the effect of longer term periods of intermittent fasting on leptin levels, we can look to two different studies examining men and women who partake in the Ramadan ritual of a month-long period of daily fasting, often consisting of 14-18 hour long fasts every day during the daylight hours for a month.

In these studies, mean leptin levels did not decrease during the period of intermittent fasting, in fact they slightly increased, and this occurred without an increase in body weight or body fat (the women actually lost body fat and had a decrease in their waist circumference).

Similar effects have also been shown to occur in men following the same fasting practice. The men in this study fasted daily for almost a month, lost body fat yet did not see any reduction in leptin levels.

As it turns out, and this is extremely important, sometimes what happens *during* a fast may not be representative of what happens *because* of a fast. In this case even though leptin levels may dip during the actual fast, the overall effect seems to be maintenance of leptin levels even with calorie restriction and a decrease on body fat levels in both men and women.

So even with the ever-increasing scientific knowledge we are gaining about the importance of leptin, using short-term flexible intermittent fasting combined with resistance training remains one of the most effective and simple ways to lose weight and reduce your body fat.

Fasting and Testosterone

Another myth about fasting is that it prevents muscle growth by decreasing testosterone levels.

In both men and women, testosterone plays a key role in health and well-being as well as in the prevention of osteoporosis. It is largely responsible for determining how much muscle mass a man (and to a lesser extent a woman) possesses and also has positive effects on a person's libido.

Athletes often use testosterone in the form of anabolic steroids as a way to improve performance, build muscle, and decrease body fat. It is considered to be a form of doping in most sports (the International Olympic Committee has banned testosterone doping).

A common belief in some athletic circles is that short periods of fasting can cause your testosterone levels to plummet.

There are a number of reasons why I was skeptical when I first heard this claim, but the most obvious to me was that I had done extensive research on testosterone for a patent I was working on back when I was employed in the supplement industry. Consequently, I knew that testosterone levels are actually highest during the morning after an overnight fast.[78] These levels will be 20-30% higher than testosterone levels found during the evening.

The other reason I was suspect of this claim is the large body of scientific research revealed that the very act of eating can decrease testosterone levels in men.

In studies where men have their testosterone levels measured during an overnight fast of 10-14 hours and then again after a standard meal of 550 calories (containing 28% protein, 26% fat, and 46% carbohydrate), the results found a decline in serum-testosterone of almost 30%. This decrease started 15 minutes after the food was consumed and continued for the full 2 hours of the study. This relationship between food intake and testosterone has been found in multiple studies in younger and older men of varying levels of fitness and body weight.[79, 80, 81, 82]

The relationship between testosterone levels and dieting has been explored in research. There is consistent evidence that mild caloric restriction (about a 15% calorie restriction) does not lead to reductions in testosterone or free testosterone in otherwise healthy males.[83] Maybe more importantly, we do know from examining large scale (over 1,000 subjects) longitudinal studies (following people for around 8 years) that gaining body fat is correlated with lower testosterone levels, and having high body fat is also correlated with having low testosterone levels.[84, 85] Luckily, the very act of losing body fat is able to restore testosterone levels back to normal levels.[86, 87]

Short-term weight loss induced by caloric restriction was shown to increase testosterone levels in abdominally obese non-diabetic and diabetic men.[88]

Based on this research, we know that being overweight and even the act of gaining weight is associated with lowered testosterone levels, mild calorie restriction is not associated with any decrease in testosterone, and losing weight can return testosterone levels back to level that would be consider normal. However, the evidence behind severe calorie restriction suggests that long-term very low-calorie diets may negatively affect testosterone.

Research has shown that a group of men undertaking large-scale caloric restriction for extended time period (~7 years) with no weight training do have lower testosterone levels than non-obese men who eat the normal American diet.[89]

However, there are a couple of points that need to be addressed with these findings. Firstly, the men following the prolonged calorie restriction diet had startlingly low levels of both fat mass and lean body mass. So, it is unclear whether the drop in testosterone was a direct result of their diet or the combination of their diet, lack of resistance training, and body composition. Secondly, their testosterone levels, while still lower than the typical men, were still within normal levels for their age.

Interestingly, we can find some very convincing answers in military research. After 8 weeks of extreme multi-stressor environments (very low-calorie diet, super high-energy expenditure, high temperatures, and extreme lack of sleep for military training) testosterone levels can drop to almost castration levels. However, a slight refeed can rapidly restore testosterone levels, and testosterone levels end up higher 5 weeks after the 8-week stressful protocol.[90] So extreme conditions including calorie deprivation can lead to reductions in testosterone, but what about fasting?

After thoroughly reviewing the available research, I found that short-term fasting does not negatively affect testosterone levels in men. However, more prolonged fasts seem to be associated with slight decreases in testosterone levels. A 58-hour fast has been noted to cause reduced morning serum testosterone measurements by the third straight morning of fasting;[91] as can fasting for 84 hours.[92] However, these measurements were still well within the normal range for healthy adults.[93] In fact, other studies have found that it takes about 9 straight days of fasting before a significant decrease in testosterone levels are observed.[94]

Research examining the effects of brief fasting (14-18 hours) over 21 days found that testosterone levels were not affected by almost a month of short-term fasting.[95]

These findings all point to the fact that short-term fasting does not have any negative effects on testosterone levels, and certainly would not cause serum testosterone levels to ever drop below normal. In fact, based on this evidence this may be one area where brief periods of fasting are actually better than prolonged dieting — since the short periods of fasting do little to disrupt testosterone levels, whereas longer more sustained periods of caloric restriction do seem to negatively affect testosterone levels in men.

However, it should be noted that in the research where longer term fasting or diets with a high level of calorie restriction did cause a reduction in testosterone, it was found that when the fasting or dieting was ceased, testosterone sensitivity was increased, and higher "rebound" levels of testosterone were observed.[96, 97]

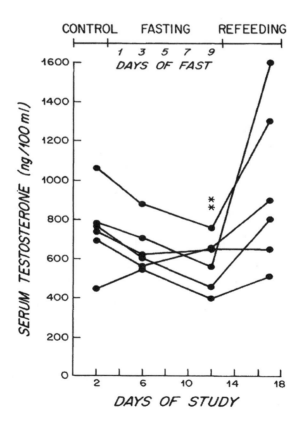

When a group of men fasted for 9 days they saw a steady decline in the testosterone levels that became significant by about day 9. However, during the re-feed period when the men were allowed to eat 1,500 calories per day (still low by most men's standards), they saw a rapid increase in their testosterone levels that exceeded their original levels for the full 5 days of the re-feed period.[98]

A similar testosterone rebound has also been found in wrestlers, whose testosterone levels decreased as they rapidly lost weight for a competition, but then rebounded higher after the competition during decreased training and increased weight.[99]

And a similar result has been found in the early periods after a fast where post-breakfast testosterone was increased in men after a fast.[100]

So far, so good. Short periods of fasting do not seem to affect testosterone levels. Longer fasts do seem to decrease testosterone, but also result in an increase in testosterone when the fast is stopped. And, perhaps most importantly, we know that losing body fat is a great way to improve overall levels of testosterone in men.

Based on these findings, it seems reasonable to suggest that if we want to use short-term fasting to lose weight we know we don't have to worry about leptin or testosterone levels. And even if we decide to use longer term fasting (longer than 24 hours) we know that both leptin and testosterone levels will return to normal once the fast is completed.

Finally, we have the myth of short periods of fasting causing elevated (or depressed) cortisol levels.

Fasting and Cortisol

Cortisol is a corticosteroid hormone, or glucocorticoid, produced by the adrenal cortex, which is part of the adrenal gland. It is usually referred to as the "stress hormone" as it's involved in your body's response to stress and anxiety.

Cortisol is released in response to various forms of stress (both physical and mental) as well as to low levels of blood glucocorticoid hormones. Its primary functions are to increase levels blood sugar through gluconeogenesis, suppress the immune system, increase blood pressure, and aid in fat, protein, and carbohydrate metabolism as a way to help your body deal with stress, illness, and injury.[101]

Cortisol is a lot like other "response systems" in your body where acute increases are usually a good thing, helping you deal with stress, but chronically elevated or depressed levels lead to health problems.

Over the last couple years cortisol has been fingered as a culprit in causing obesity, specifically through a speculative link to belly fat. And, just like anything else that has been labeled "bad," it has been rumored that if you don't eat every couple of hours you would cause your cortisol levels to jump. This "jump" has been associated with a whole host of problems other than increasing body fat, including the rumor that, "If you don't eat every couple of hours your cortisol will get very high and it will destroy your muscle mass."

The truth is cortisol secretion is vitally important to your overall health. Short periods of increased cortisol secretion are useful, such as the increased cortisol in the morning that helps liberate body fat to be used as a fuel, while prolonged cortisol increases may increase vulnerability to immuno-suppression, and to autoimmune-related and metabolic disorders.[102]

Since proper cortisol secretion is extremely important to overall health, it is definitely worthwhile examining how fasting affects cortisol.

In direct opposition to the cortisol scaremongering we find in the media, the consistent finding in the research on fasting is that there is very little or no change in cortisol levels in response to a short period of fasting. This is true for both a short 24-hour fast[103] as well as after 72 hours of fasting.[104] While research has shown that 5 straight days of fasting can cause a 1.8-fold increase in the 24-hour endogenous cortisol production rate[105], it has also been found that even 2 weeks of fasting every other day (36-hour fasts) did not negatively affect cortisol levels.[106]

The funny thing is, we have known for more than 4 decades that increased cortisol is a phenomenon that is regularly found in obesity.[107] And, that there is a direct correlation between the amount of body fat you have and your circulating cortisol levels. The inactive form of cortisol (cortisone) from the blood is converted to active cortisol by enzymes found within adipose tissue.[108] This seems to be one of the mechanisms by which obesity can cause elevated cortisol levels.

We have also known that treating obesity with very low-calorie diets causes a decrease in serum cortisol. So, being overweight increases cortisol, the actual act of fasting doesn't make it go up or down (at least when fasting for less than 72 hours), and losing weight will help return cortisol to normal? Sounds like even more reason to try short periods of fasting for weight loss.

This isn't to say that everyone's cortisol levels are immune to weight loss. 72 hours of fasting has been found to increase cortisol levels in extremely lean (18% body fat) women, and chronic strenuous exercise has been shown to cause long term increases in cortisol secretion.[109]

The truly amazing thing is that while delving into these common nutritional myths I began to find more and more health benefits that are associated with taking brief breaks from eating. It seems that fasting can have many positive health effects beyond simply helping you lose weight and burn body fat.

But What about Breakfast?

Probably one of the biggest concerns people have when it comes to fasting (after worrying about their metabolism "crashing") has to be the idea of missing a breakfast, and I can see why. For close to 3 decades now, nutritionists and nutritional texts have been recommending breakfast as an important part of healthy eating habits, often quoting the "most important meal of the day" marketing mantra.[110]

There is one major problem with the idea of missing breakfast — it's not actually possible. The reality is breakfast is the first meal of the day no matter when you eat it. After all, breakfast is a two-part word, "break" and "fast." The meaning is literally "breaking a fast." So by the purest definition of the word, your first meal after waking up, no matter how many hours after you wake up, counts as breakfast because this is the meal that "breaks the fast."

It is only for research and marketing purposes that breakfast is labeled as a meal that is eaten in the morning right after you've rolled out of bed.

Of course, this still leaves us with questions such as, "How long after waking up is my first meal still considered breakfast? Is it 30 minutes after waking up? 1 hour? 2 hours? What if I'm a shift working and I start my day at 10pm? Does my first meal at 11pm count as breakfast?" Of course, none of these questions are answered in the scientific literature as the answers will not fit into the neat and tidy marketing story of what breakfast is supposed to be.

Based on long-term research it is true that people who regularly ate breakfast had a "better BMI," weighed less, and had less health risks than those who regularly skipped breakfast.[111] The problem is, however, the association of breakfast eating and weight is complicated by MAJOR lifestyle confounders. For instance, breakfast consumers were more likely than breakfast non-consumers to be older, female, white, nonsmokers, regular exercisers, and trying to control their weight.

So, people who are active and health conscious tend to be the ones who eat breakfast. Which begs the question—is this because eating breakfast is in fact healthy and promotes a healthy lifestyle, or is it because breakfast is currently being marketed as healthy and therefore those seeking to be healthier start eating breakfast? It is also likely that people with high BMIs favor skipping breakfast in an attempt to lose weight.[112]

Despite the correlations between weight and eating trends and all the semantic arguments about what is and isn't breakfast, we must look to research to provide us with some evidence to help us rate the importance of breakfast, and to find possible mechanisms that would account for breakfast's overall effect on health and weight.

After reviewing the total body of research on breakfast, one thing becomes startlingly clear—the amount of food you eat at breakfast is strongly correlated to your overall daily intake. Or put more simply—as calories consumed at breakfast go up, so does overall calorie intake for the day.[113, 114, 115, 116]

The second thing that also reoccurs across multiple research studies is that the people who skip (delay) breakfast select more calorically dense foods later in the day than do those who regularly eat breakfast. The argument "skipping breakfast leads to eating more during the day" is technically backed by research.[117] At first glance this could seem as a major negative of delaying your first meal, however, the critical piece of information that usually fails to get reported is this same research shows the amount of "extra" calories breakfast skippers eat at lunch and dinner is not enough to make up for the calories lost by skipping breakfast.

In other words, even though breakfast skippers eat slightly more calories at dinner and lunch, they still eat less total calories over the entire day.

So while skipping eating in the traditional "breakfast" period may lead to eating more calories at other meals, the result is still typically a reduction in overall calorie intake. Thus, we can conclude that skipping breakfast does not lead to eating more total calories.[118]

The other prevailing argument for the importance of breakfast is that skipping breakfast leads to increased snacking throughout the rest of the day.

The typical warning against skipping breakfast is something like this: *"The last thing anyone should do is skip breakfast. Otherwise, you'll be eating something even worse later on — candy bars and potato chips — because you're starving."*

This is the common thinking when it comes to breakfast. Skipping breakfast means eating crap later in the day. So, the question becomes, "Is this true, and does it matter?"

When it comes to the benefits of breakfast and weight loss, we can turn to the research utilizing calorie restricted diets that either did, or did not, skip breakfast. In this research, both diets caused equal weight loss. In other words, research shows that skipping breakfast has no effect on weight loss results when the diets have equal amounts of calorie restriction.[119]

The reason this particular study is of interest is because the researchers of this study did note that snacking was increased in the non-breakfast eaters.

The authors wrote that, *"The other major advantage of eating breakfast was a greater reduction in unplanned, impulsive snacks."*

I would argue that since total weight loss was the same, and that skipping breakfast was even associated with better totally body fat loss, this statement could be rewritten to say: *"The major advantage of skipping breakfast was a greater ability to partake in unplanned impulsive snacks and still lose significant amounts of weight and body fat."*

So, the importance of traditional "breakfast" for weight loss seems to be minimal at best, but that doesn't mean we should all write off breakfast. Just because breakfast isn't the "most important meal of the day," doesn't mean it can't be your "most enjoyable meal of the day."

Short-term fasting doesn't have to mean you ever miss breakfast. If you choose to, you can arrange your fasts so that you never miss a breakfast. You can reap all the benefits of fasting while still eating breakfast every day, or 5 days out of the week, or only on weekends. It's completely up to you.

The Health Benefits of Fasting

After reviewing all the research I could find on fasting, I was astonished at all the health benefits that short-term fasting can offer. Do you remember in the late 1990s when the Mediterranean diet became all the rage? The idea behind the diet was based on research conducted in the Greek island of Crete. The research suggested that the diet of the Mediterranean region was superior to the North American diet.

On average, the population of Crete was healthier than North Americans, with less incidence of cardiovascular or heart disease. Researchers attributed this improved level of health to a high daily intake of whole grains, fruits, vegetables, and olive oil.

This theory made good sense, as these are all accepted "healthy" foods. However, recent reviews by a group of researchers at the University of Crete School of Medicine suggest that one very important factor was left out of this research. In the Greek Orthodox Christian Church, there are some very lengthy fasting traditions.[120]

The Orthodox Church specifies a combination of dietary restrictions and fasting for a total of between 180 and 200 days out of every year. While this is by no means conclusive evidence, it did suggest that a very healthy group of people were not only consuming plentiful amounts of healthy foods, but also took part in routine periods of fasting.[121]

By the time I had finished my research, I had reached the conclusion that short-term (1 to 3 days) intermittent (never in a row) fasting, was not only an effective and easy way to cut calories and thus lose unwanted body fat, but it was also associated with many amazing health benefits.

The science of nutrition is an ever-evolving entity. Every month, hundreds of scientific publications are added to the constantly growing body of literature. This being said, it is a scientific mistake to simply "cherry pick" the latest research. You must have a solid understanding of the entire history of the science before you can accurately analyze it.

In fact, the very principles of *Eat Stop Eat* emerged from three of perhaps the most renowned scientific hypotheses in all of nutrition.

1   The "thrifty genotype" hypothesis of J.V. Neel.[122] While the interpretation of this research has changed over the years, and is often misunderstood (at the early stages this theory was even used to support the dreaded "starvation mode"); the theory has now developed into the simple idea that evolution has favored the survival of individuals

genetically equipped with a good appetite and the ability to store surplus calories as fat. The importance of this hypothesis is that it answered the question, "Why do we get fat in the first place?" The answer being, "To increase survival by making sure we are able to store energy in the form of fat."

2   The "glucose fatty acid cycle" by P.J. Randle, et al.[123] This hypothesis led to the discovery that free fatty acids from our fat stores and the glucose in our blood literally compete as a fuel source in our bodies, and that our body fat will always win this competition. While this is a very scientifically complex hypothesis, its importance cannot be ignored since it led to the discovery that by burning fat as a fuel (like when you are fasting) you are able to decrease the need for protein breakdown (you won't burn muscle as a fuel). In other words, the very act of burning body fat preserves muscle mass.

3   The "feast and famine cycle" by Rabinowitz and Zierler.[124] This was the first scientific theory that clearly outlined the relationship between insulin and growth hormone, and is the reason why growth hormone gets a "starring role" in the explanation of how Eat Stop Eat causes you to lose body fat without losing muscle. The "feast and famine cycle" also helps to explain why we burn body fat while we are fasting, and burn calories from our food when we are eating.

These three seemingly unrelated theories were all developed in the mid-nineteen-sixties, and all three were considered very controversial at the time. What I found most interesting about these theories was that most people studying nutrition did so under the assumption that we needed to be constantly eating, so nobody had really thought to look at these three theories as a whole.

In fact, it wasn't until I looked at these three theories with the idea of fasting that I was able to put them together into one unifying theory that helps explain many of the discoveries currently being made in today's nutritional sciences. It was these three scientific principles that led to the realization that it made perfect sense that we store energy as body fat. It also led me to realize that it was entirely possible to get rid of this body fat while not losing our muscle mass; and finally, that the special relationship between growth hormone and insulin played an intricate role in this process.

It was this revelation that led me to review all the research I could find on the metabolic effects of short-term fasting. By the time I was finished, I had found that in a very impressive volume of published peer reviewed scientific studies, short-term intermittent fasting has been shown to have the following health benefits:

- Decreased body fat & body weight
- Maintenance of skeletal muscle mass
- Decreased blood glucose levels
- Decreased insulin levels & increased insulin sensitivity
- Increased lipolysis & fat oxidation
- Increased uncoupling protein-3 mRNA
- Increased norepinephrine & epinephrine levels
- Increased glucagon levels
- Increased growth hormone levels
- Decreased food related stress

- Decreased chronic systemic inflammation
- Increased cellular cleansing

Quite a list, I'm sure you will agree. What is even more amazing is that many of the benefits were found after as little as 24-hours of fasting!

From experience in the supplement industry, I can tell you that if you could make a pill with all these claims, you would easily have a 100-million-dollar-a-year product. You'd probably also win a Nobel Prize. These claims are that impressive!

Now that we have debunked many of the negative stories about fasting, and have discovered that fasting can have all of these aforementioned beneficial effects, it raises the question—should we all be fasting?

In order to find the answer, let's take a closer look at some of these health benefits.

Decreased Insulin Levels & Increased Insulin Sensitivity

Insulin is one of the most important hormones in your body. Every nutrition, medicine, and physiology textbook has at least one chapter devoted entirely to the effects that insulin has on your physiology.

Whenever you eat any type of food your blood insulin levels increase. While certain macronutrients raise insulin more than others (protein and carbohydrates having a much larger effect than fat), almost all of the food we eat contains *at least* two of the macronutrients; thus, it is fairly safe to say that ANYTHING you eat that contains calories will raise your insulin levels to some degree.

This increased amount of circulating insulin drives the storage of nutrients within your body. In other words, insulin is the primary signal that tells your body to store the energy from your food as body fat and glycogen. Insulin is the key that drives glucose (sugar) out of your blood and into your fat and muscle cells.

When insulin levels are high, you are in storage mode—plain and simple. What's more, when insulin is elevated, you are unable to release fat from your fat stores. The key thing to remember is when your insulin is high; your body fat isn't going anywhere.

The problem with insulin lies in the fact that most of us are eating too much too often. As a result, we have chronically elevated insulin levels. Chronically elevated insulin levels are associated with the development of insulin resistance, diabetes, inflammation, cardiovascular disease, and some forms of cancer.

Many popular diets, such as *The Zone* and *The South Beach Diet*, are based around the idea of controlling your insulin levels. These diets attempt to help you accomplish this by instructing you to eat small frequent meals that have a lesser effect on your blood sugar levels.

While eating frequent small meals, or meals with a low "glycemic index" (a measure of the meal's effect on blood sugar) may help you "control" or "even out" your insulin levels, this is not always the case. In fact, having very high levels of insulin can actually make something appear to have a low "glycemic index," making someone think their insulin levels are low when in fact they are actually quite high.

It is perfectly possible to overeat and increase your weight and body fat while keeping your insulin levels "stable."

This is where fasting is different. Fasting for as little as 24 hours has been shown to drastically reduce your insulin levels.[125] This is especially important because in order to burn body fat, insulin levels must be very low. Simply "evening them out" may not be enough, especially if this evening out of your blood sugar levels is due to chronically high insulin levels.

In research conducted on people who fasted for 72-hours, plasma insulin levels dropped dramatically, reaching a level that was less than half of its initial levels. What is even more impressive is that 70% of this reduction happened during the first 24-hours of fasting.[126, 127]

In other words, a 24-hour fast has a more dramatic effect on reducing insulin than all of the insulin based diets, like low-carb or frequent meal timing, could ever hope to have. If you actually want to bring your insulin levels down, the best tool you have is short-term fasting.

By fasting once or twice a week you create small periods of time where insulin levels are allowed to become very low. Combine this with the periods where you are eating normally and insulin levels are elevated and you recreate the balance of low and high insulin that is needed for the maintenance of good health and a desirable body weight.

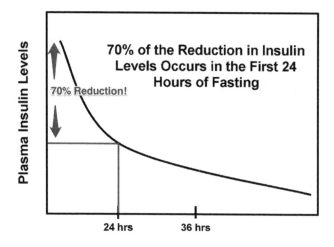

Hours Spent in the Fastened State

As little as 24 hours of fasting can cause a
marked decrease in circulating insulin levels

Insulin sensitivity refers to how well (or how poorly) our bodies are able to respond to the hormone insulin. Individuals who are insulin resistant tend to have higher baseline insulin levels because the body has to release more insulin to try and overcome this resistance.

Both intermittent fasting and long-term caloric restriction have been shown to cause an improved insulin sensitivity as measured by something called HOMA-IR, which stands for "Homeostasis Model Assessment of Insulin Resistance"[128] and by another method called "the euglycemic clamp."

Turner and colleagues first proposed the homeostatic model assessment (HOMA) as a way to measure insulin sensitivity in the late 1970s. This approach involves measuring fasting levels of plasma glucose and fasting levels of plasma insulin.[129, 130]

The "euglycemic insulin clamp" is another method of deter-mining insulin sensitivity and is currently considered the gold-standard model in research studies. Like the measure-ments for the HOMA-IR test, the euglycemic insulin clamp is typically conducted in subjects after a 10 to 12-hour over-night fast.

Measuring insulin sensitivity can be difficult since insulin sensitivity can vary depending on the tissue in your body. So, your liver may have a different level of sensitivity than your skeletal muscle or your body fat, but in general both of these measurements are considered good markers of overall insulin status.

What we do know from studying insulin sensitivity is that chronically low insulin sensitivity (called insulin resistance) is a common metabolic abnormality that you find in many different medical disorders, including type 2 diabetes and obesity.

Luckily, dietary induced weight loss, with or without exer-cise, can significantly improve insulin sensitivity in both men and women.[131, 132] It is also worth noting that older women derived as much benefit as the younger women.[133]

So, using a 24-hour fast once or twice a week is an excel-lent way for people with low levels of insulin sensitivity to improve their insulin sensitivity, especially when combined with exercise and weight loss.

Decreased Blood Glucose Levels

Blood sugar concentration or (blood glucose) is the amount of glucose (sugar) present in your blood at any given moment. Our bodies are remarkably effective at maintaining our blood sugar within a very tight range. Throughout the typical 24-hour cycles of eating, digestion, and fasting, the amount of glucose in your blood is generally maintained within a range of 70-140 mg/dL (3.9-7.8 mmol/L) as long as you are healthy.

The problem occurs when we are constantly eating, or even worse, constantly overeating. When we are constantly eating, our bodies struggle to keep up with the continuous supply of glucose and we run the risk of chronically elevated blood glucose levels and the long-term health consequences that are associated with this state. This problem becomes even worse in situations of obesity and inflammation.

Prolonged excess blood glucose is a key factor that is pro-aging through both direct and indirect effects.[134] In clinical research we have seen that giving animals really high blood glucose levels via infusion (a scientific way of recreating an episode of overfeeding) led to a decrease in antioxidants, increased liver oxidative stress, and systemic inflammatory response.[135]

Luckily, even an extremely short period of fasting (12-18 hours) is enough to allow our body to regulate our blood glucose and return them to their normal fasting level.[136]

So simply by taking a brief break from eating, we are able to give our metabolisms enough time to slowly correct our blood glucose levels; by reducing our body fat and the amount of food we eat, we create an environment where our bodies can once again easily regulate our blood glucose levels.

Increased Lipolysis and Fat Burning

There are a few very important steps in the process of burning fat. First, your fat has to be "released" from your adipose tissue (fancy name for body fat). Scientists call this lipolysis, and it involves the process of releasing the fatty acids that make up your fat, and moving these fatty acids into your bloodstream so they can eventually be burned as a fuel by your muscles and internal organs.

After a series of steps that allow these fatty acids to get to the mitochondria in your muscles (the metabolic "engine" of every cell in your body) these fatty acids go through a process called beta oxidation. This is the final step of fat burning— once this has happened your body fat has now been used for energy. It is gone and it cannot come back.

Let's review that quickly. Fat must be released from its storage spot (our body fat), transported through your system, and get to a cellular engine where it will be burned (typically in your muscles or organs).

While we are resting, our muscles are a major contributor to our metabolic rate (along with our organs). During a fasted state, our muscles begin to switch over and start oxidizing fatty acids from our body fat as a fuel. In other words, when we fast, our muscles turn into fat burning machines. Despite the common assumption, our bodies DO NOT attack our muscles and use them for fuel when we are fasting. In fact, quite the opposite happens—our muscles turn into the machine that actively burns our body fat.

A 24-hour period of fasting shifts your body from the fed state to the fasted state, which causes large increases in both lipolysis (fat release) and fat oxidation (fat burning). Simply put, fasting allows your body to take a break from storing fat, and start burning it. (Which, of course, is the EXACT reason we store body fat in the first place!)

During short-term fasting, free fatty acids start to be released from your body fat as soon as you are done burning the calories that you consumed during your last meal. Depending on the size of the meal, this can happen anywhere from 2-6 hours into a fast. After this point, the amount of free fatty acids entering your blood continue to increase as does the amount of body fat being oxidized for energy. By about the 12 to 14-hour mark, you begin to burn predominantly body fat as your main fuel source.

Probably the most revealing information in the research I have read was found in studies published by a group of scientists from the University of Texas, Medical Branch at Galveston. It examined how short-term fasting affects fat and sugar metabolism in our bodies.

After only 24-hours of fasting, the amount of fat being released from people's fat stores (lipolysis) and the amount being burned for fuel (oxidation) had been significantly increased by over 50%. This is a very significant increase in fat burning in a relatively short period of time.

This also helps illustrate how even short periods of fasting (approximately 24-hours), can have profound effects on our body's ability to burn body fat. In fact, recent research has illustrated that fasting actually does a better job than exercising when it comes to turning on some key fat burning hormones.

The recently discovered hormone adipose triglyceride lipase (ATGL) is responsible for the very first step of released fat from your fat stores.[137] It is ATGL in combination with another enzyme called hormone sensitive lipase that governs the ability of adipose tissue to mobilize fat stores to be used as a fuel. And, it just so happens that

short periods of fasting have an incredibly potent effect on ATGL, even more so than the effects of exercise.[138] Short periods of fasting are able to cause a rapid release of FFAs from your fat stores.

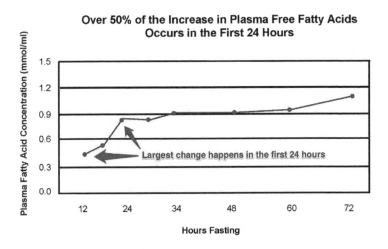

Over 50% of the Increase in Plasma Free Fatty Acids Occurs in the First 24 Hours

Even with short periods of fasting, there is an increased availability of body fat to be burned as fuel

More evidence of the fat burning effects of fasting comes from something called uncoupling protein-3.

Uncoupling protein-3 is a very important protein found in our muscles that is associated with fat burning. When fat-burning increases so does the amount of Uncoupling protein-3 in our muscles.

Amazing research has shown that as little as 15-hours into a fast, the gene expression (amount of protein being built) for uncoupling protein-3 increases fivefold![139]

This same research also illustrates that the gene expression for uncoupling protein-3 (UCP3) continues to increase even up to the 40-hour mark of a fast.

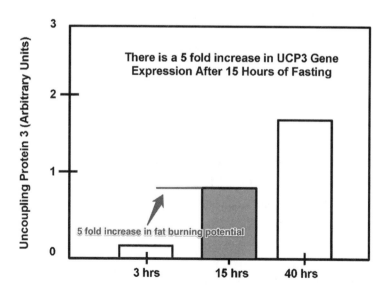

Hours Spent in the Fasted State

As fat burning increases, so do levels of UCP3

This is very important research because fat burning should be the goal of every diet. You should never lose weight without losing fat. We should forget the idea of "losing weight" and focus on "losing body fat."

Increased Glucagon Levels

If we consider fed and fasted to be the yin and yang of metabolism, then the hormonal equivalent to fed and fasted could be thought of as the opposing effects of the hormones insulin and glucagon.

Insulin is the dominant hormone in the fed state, which causes you to store food calories in the form of fat and glycogen. Glucagon is one of the dominant hormones in the fasted state that causes fat burning.

Quick review:

Insulin = Fat storage

Glucagon = Fat burning

Both hormones are secreted from your pancreas, and while the primary role of insulin is to maintain your blood sugar levels while you are in the fed state, the primary role of glucagon is to maintain your blood sugar levels while you are in the fasted state.

Insulin maintains your blood sugar levels by telling your body to store extra sugar when your blood sugar levels run the risk of getting too high, while glucagon tells your body to release extra sugar from its stores when your blood sugar runs the risk of getting too low.

Glucagon has some amazing effects on the human body beyond maintaining our blood sugar levels including increasing fat burning, decreasing the production of cholesterol, and increasing the release of extra fluids from the body.

Because of the typical way we eat, we spend almost all of our time in an "insulin dominant" metabolism (remember insulin = fat storage). By adding fasting into your lifestyle, you allow your body to revert back to a natural balance between an "insulin dominant" metabolism and a "glucagon dominant" metabolism.

Increased Epinephrine and Norepinephrine Levels

Epinephrine and norepinephrine are fight-or-flight hormones, often called adrenalin and noradrenalin, or collectively, "catecholamines." They are released from the adrenal glands during periods of stress; including times when food is absent (such as fasting) and during intense exercise.

When they are released into the bloodstream, the catecholamines trigger the release of glucose from energy stores, and increase fat burning. They also make you feel awake and alert.

Fasting increases the amounts of both these hormones in your blood. This is your body's way of maintaining your blood sugar levels and increasing your fuel supply by helping to release fatty acids from your fat stores.

Now, you wouldn't want your catecholamine levels increased all the time, nor do you want them to be drastically elevated.

Like all hormones there is a healthy range for your catechol-amines and having them extremely low or extremely high for long periods of time is associated with negative aspects of health.

However, the occasional increases in catecholamine levels you get through both exercise and fasting will help you with your fat loss efforts. It's only a small increase, but it may be partly responsible for the increased levels of concentration and alert-ness that some people report during both fasting and exercise.

Increased Growth Hormone Levels

Growth hormone is an extremely important hormone which throughout evolution has had the responsibility of maintain-ing growth and lean body mass during the times when food is sparse. You've probably heard of growth hormone (or GH) since it has been getting a lot of press these days. Rumor mills are buzzing that many top-level Hollywood celebrities are taking growth hormone because it helps burn fat, build muscle, and supposedly has "anti-aging" effects.

Many supplement companies are scrambling around trying to find anything that will allow them to say their products can increase growth hormone.

The ironic thing I learned from all this research is that if you want large increases in the amount of growth hormone released in your body, all you have to do is fast.

The secretion of growth hormone in your body can be stim-ulated by fasting, sleep, exercise, and sex hormones such as testosterone and estradiol.[140, 141]

Research has shown that short-term fasting can result in a six-fold increase in growth hormone levels.[142, 143, 144] Considering that an increase in GH of nearly 3-fold (roughly the amount you'd find during sleep or exercise) is able to increase fat burning, it becomes evident that even short periods of fasting can drastically increase fat burning in men and women.[145]

The fact is fasting can cause very large increases in the amount of circulating growth hormone in both men and women, young and old. In other words, the same growth hormone that celebrities, bodybuilders and fitness models pay thousands of dollars for on the black market can be easily had for free, just by fasting!

24 Hour Profiles of Serum GH Concentrations

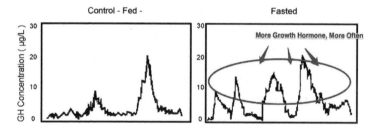

Fasting increases growth hormone

The rumor that taking growth hormone helps in the process of burning fat, building muscle, and increasing metabolism is actually supported by research.[146, 147, 148] However, the amazing connection between growth hormone and fasting has nothing to do with injecting growth hormone.

It was more than a half-century ago that we first uncovered the powerful role that growth hormone has on fasting metabolism.[149] Fasting triggers the "growth hormone response" and this response is what prevents you from losing muscle while you fast.[150, 151] In fact, research has shown that when people fast and do not have any growth hormone (its release was blocked in the study), there is an increase in protein loss by about 50%![152] Yet further evidence that growth hormone is an incredibly important part of the fasting process.

Another point to consider is that growth hormone is the only anabolic hormone that is actually increased by fasting. And, since your muscle is largely responsible for your metabolism, growth hormone also plays a large part in keeping your metabolism elevated while you are fasting.[153]

Growth hormone also plays an important role in maintaining healthy blood glucose levels while you are fasting. By increasing the amount of fat you're burning as a fuel, it reduces the need to use glucose as a fuel source. To put it rather simply, as your fat burning goes up, your sugar burning goes down. This is important for two reasons. It keeps your blood glucose levels stable, and it is also part of the reason why you do not lose muscle mass while you fast (remember the "feast famine cycle" we talked about earlier). By lowering the amount of glucose that is needed by your body, it prevents your body from breaking down your skeletal muscles in order to make new glucose.[154]

Not only does growth hormone prevent you from losing muscle while you fast, it is also vitally important in the process of releasing your stored fat so it can be burned for energy. It upregulates key enzymes allowing for fat, that was released from your fat stores, to be brought into your muscle to be burned as a fuel.[155, 156]

It is easy to think of this as a sort of cyclical relationship. Eating prevents the release of growth hormone, while fasting promotes the release of growth hormone. Eating prevents the release and use of body fat as a fuel, while fasting promotes the release and use of body fat as a fuel.

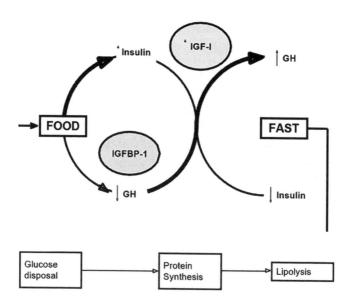

Here's another interesting point about growth hormone: People who have high levels of body fat typically have lower levels of growth hormone. This is especially apparent in people with a high amount of abdominal fat.[157]

Not only does being obese tend to lower growth hormone levels, the very act of overeating can cause a rapid suppression of growth hormone. In a study published in 2011, it was found that as little as 3 days of overeating (the people in the study ate about 4,000 calories per day) suppressed growth hormone levels by as much as 80%.[158] So being overweight, carrying a large amount of fat in or around your abdomen, and the very act of overeating (even for a couple days) is able to suppress growth hormone release. Luckily, weight loss and the act of fasting are able to improve the release of growth hormone in obese people.[159]

While an obese person may not release as much growth hormone as a lean person during a fast, as they lose weight through fasting the amount of GH they release during a fast will continue to increase, until they reach the point where they release the same amount as a lean person.

This growth hormone response to fasting is so important that some researchers have actually argued that in the yin and yang of fed and fasted, it is actually growth hormone and not glucagon that is the dominant hormone in the fasted state because it causes fat burning and preserves your muscle mass.[160]

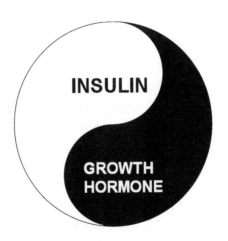

FED – Insulin Dominant Metabolism

FASTED – Growth Hormone Dominant Metabolism

Growth hormone is also tied to the aging process. Your highest levels of growth hormone will occur during your young adult years.[161] Then, beginning in early adulthood, GH declines at a slow steady rate leading to GH deficiency in some older populations.[162, 163] These declining levels of GH have been correlated with the weight you gain in older age, as well as reduced insulin sensitivity and even muscle loss.[164]

So with all these amazing benefits of growth hormone, you may be wondering why everyone just doesn't inject themselves with GH? Truthfully people do inject themselves with growth hormone, but doing so is involved with its own set of risks. Having growth hormone elevated chronically is not desirable, as chronic elevations of GH can keep you in a perpetual fat burning state. While this may sound fantastic, this also means you are in a perpetual state of NOT burning carbohydrates as a fuel.

As a result, people using GH may risk the occurrence of insulin resistance since their muscles have no real reason to be insulin sensitive if they are simply burning fat all day long.[165, 166] So prolonged periods of increased GH is not our goal. Instead, we're looking for the occasional fasting induced increase (a once-in-a-while spike in GH levels rather than prolonged, chronic elevations).

Another reason why fasting-induced increases in GH are preferred over injected growth hormone is that research has shown that fasting actually sensitizes your body to the fat burning effects of growth hormone. In other words, growth hormone causes more fat loss in the fasted state than if you injected it when you weren't fasting.[167]

Another interesting fact about GH is that you need to be fasting, not just dieting, to get its full effect. A 5-day fast (much longer than I would ever recommend) significantly increases spontaneous 24-hour GH secretion, whereas 4 days of following a very-low calorie diet does not have the same effect.[168] Even more interesting is that adding exercise into your weight loss program seems to increase GH levels more than just a diet alone.[169]

So the three best ways to get natural increases in growth hormone are fasting, exercise, and deep sleep—three things that we can all agree are generally associated with good health, lower body fat, and possibly even an extended life-span.

The key to growth hormone isn't to have as much as possible, since too much or too little of any hormone in your body can have negative effects. Instead, by fasting you can "reset" the balance between insulin and growth hormone. What's even better is that as you lose weight, your body becomes better at releasing GH when you are fasting and when you are exercising.[170] (Talk about win-win situation!)

It is important to note that while growth hormone does have pronounced fat burning effects in the body, it is by no means a "cure all" or "miracle hormone." It is just one of the many benefits of fasting that all work in connection with each other to help you lose weight.

When it comes to building muscle, some people have speculated that the increases in growth hormone caused by fasting can actually help you increase your lean muscle mass. Unfortunately, this is typical fitness world conjecture that is not fully supported by research. While this is a very interesting theory and GH has been shown to stimulate protein synthesis and repress protein breakdown, to date there is little evidence to suggest this leads to long-term muscle gain.[171] In fact, in a recent publication by renowned researcher Michael Rennie it was stated that:

> "So far, no robust credible study has been able to show clear effects of either medium to long-term GH administration, alone or in combination with a variety of training protocols or anabolic steroids, on muscle protein synthesis, mass, or strength.[172]"

The bottom line is most of us spend way too much time in an insulin dominant metabolism, and would benefit from a fast or two a week to help balance our insulin dominant metabolism with our growth hormone dominant metabolism. That being said, as with all hormones, balance is the key. We are not chasing prolonged elevated levels of growth hormone, nor should we have unrealistic expectations of what we can achieve with our fasting.

Fasting will help us lose body fat, and growth hormone plays a major role in this process (you really can't burn body fat without GH), but we cannot expect fasting to have steroid-like effects or be some miracle hormone that will cause us to lose fat AND build massive muscles.

Increased Weight Loss and Increased Fat Loss

As you can see, fasting sets you up perfectly for fat loss and weight loss. Metabolically it prepares your body by increasing all of the hormones necessary to increase fat burning.

Added to that, it creates a large energy deficit without creating a reduction in your metabolic rate, so your body has virtually no choice but to start burning body fat for energy.

Research shows that you will lose between one-and-a-half to three-pounds every time you fast.[173, 174] THIS IS NOT ALL FAT. Much of this is extra body water being lost (insulin causes you to store extra water, so when insulin is low, you tend to lose water), and a reduction in the mass of digesting food that is usually in your stomach and intestines. You are also losing fat, but this is a slow and steady process. Depending on your size (taller, bigger people lose more), most diets see a loss of one to two pounds of fat per week — at best. Adding short-term fasting into your lifestyle will have the same effect (just without the daily dieting).

Body Weight Changes During 24 Days of Intermittent Fasting

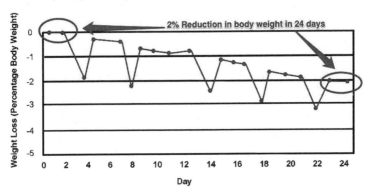

Occasional periods of fasting result in weight loss

People in studies who have used short-term fasting as a weight loss method managed to lose more weight in a 10-week period than people on a very low-calorie diet.

Even more impressive is that the people who used fasting as a method of weight control maintained most of their weight loss over the course of an entire year. This is very different from the people who were on more traditional low-calorie and very low-calorie diets, who tended to regain all of the weight one year after their initial diet.[175]

Another major benefit of fasting is that it can be used to maintain a new lower weight. If fasting twice a week helped you reduce your weight, then fasting once a week may be able to help you maintain that new weight for years on end. And, if fasting once a week was able to help you reduce your weight, then you may be able to maintain your new weight while only fasting once every 7 to 10 days (as long as you don't raise your calorie intake or decrease your activity level).

Decreased Inflammation

If you were to read through the top ten medical journals right now, I would be willing to bet that almost all of them would have at least one article on something called "chronic systemic inflammation." As our understanding of this metabolic process increases, we are beginning to realize just how detrimental chronic inflammation can be to our health and well-being.

Inflammation is a complicated part of our physiology. Our bodies unleash something called an "acute inflammation response" as a result of injury. With the acute inflammation response, the body reacts to a harmful stimulus like a bee sting by inflaming or swelling the area around the harmed tissue in an attempt to remove whatever is harming it (in this case the bee's stinger). Once this is achieved and the harmful agent is eliminated, the inflammation is reduced and the process of tissue repair begins.

This response is a protective attempt to remove the painful stimulus and to initiate the healing process. Without inflammation, wounds and infections would never heal. So, in this sense it could be said that acute inflammation is a good thing that is essential to the proper maintenance of the human body. In fact, this type of inflammation is even involved in the recovery process from exercise. However, chronic systemic inflammation can be damaging to the human body.

If acute inflammation is the body's physiological response to harmful stimuli, then chronic inflammation is the body's response to the chronic harmful stimuli of over-nutrition and excess body fat. In essence, the extra fat and the enlarged hypertrophied fat cells that accompany it are the "harmful stimuli" that is causing the inflammation; only our bodies cannot get rid of the fat with the inflammation response and thus will stay inflamed as long as the extra fat is still present. Now, when it comes to enlarged fat cells causing inflammation, some people seem to be more susceptible than others,[176] but the end result is almost always the same. High levels of body fat eventually become associated with chronic low-grade inflammation.

This type of prolonged whole body (systemic) inflammation is associated with many disease states including: rheumatoid arthritis, hypertension, atherosclerosis, fatty liver, and asthma as well as insulin resistance, cardiovascular disease, diabetes, and even the aging process itself.[177, 178] For this reason, chronic inflammation is believed to be the link between obesity and many of the life threatening diseases that are associated being overweight.

Chronic inflammation has even been linked to many of the causes and risks for the development of cancer.[179] Surprisingly, this inflammation-cancer link was suggested as far back as the late 1800s when German Pathologist Rudolf Virchow stated:

> "Chronic irritation which is manifested by a chronic inflammation is a key promoter of cancer."

Chronic inflammation is widely observed in obesity and overeating. In fact, excess body fat is the major source of chronic inflammation in the obese (as opposed to some of the other lifestyle factors of obesity).[180] Combine this with the fact that both insulin and blood glucose can increase inflammation in a dose-response manner (the higher the chronic levels of insulin, the higher the inflammation) and we can see why obesity or even just periods of overeating can lead to so many life-threatening diseases.

In people who are obese we commonly see many elevated markers of inflammation including: interleukin-6, tumor necrosis factor alpha, C-reactive protein, insulin, blood glucose, leptin, and interleukin-18.[181, 182] Luckily, short-term fasting—and more specifically, calorie restriction and weight loss — reduces many of these markers of chronic inflammation.[183, 184, 185]

Short-term fasting, and the caloric restriction it causes, is able to greatly reduce markers of chronic inflammation through many of the benefits we have already talked about (including the reduction of insulin levels) as well as some we have not (including the manipulation of hormones like adopenectin and ghrelin).

Not only this, but by following the *Eat Stop Eat* lifestyle of flexible intermittent fasting and resistance training (which can also reduce many markers of inflammation[186]), you get rid of two main causes of inflammation—excess body fat and overeating. And keep in mind, it's not just the loss of body fat that is having an effect, eating less and exercising also have direct effects on reducing inflammation,[187] so by doing all three you create a synergistic "attack" on inflammation.

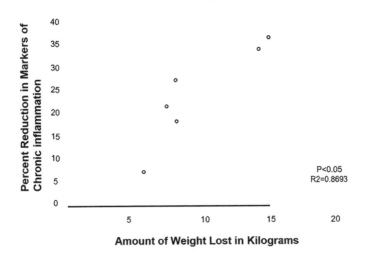

The Anti-Inflammatory Effects of Caloric Restriction and Weight Loss

Keeping inflammation under control is important for a number of reasons, including overall health and your ability to build muscle. Even a small increase in chronic inflammation can increase the risk of muscle strength loss and cause a decrease in your ability to build muscle.[188] In fact, chronic inflammation has been implicated as part of the cause of the muscle loss that occurs with aging (known as sarcopenia).[189, 190]

When you consider the fact that chronic inflammation has been suggested to be a major cause of the aging process (this has been called the "Molecular Inflammatory Theory of Aging"), this could make fasting not only your best weapon for weight loss, but also your easiest weapon for combating chronic inflammation and possibly increasing your lifespan.

Increased Cellular "Cleansing"

To truly understand the long-term health benefits of fasting, we need to look into a unique process within the human body called "autophagy."

Autophagy is a process within your body that is responsible for degrading damaged and defective organelles, cell membranes, and proteins. Basically, it's your body's internal "maintenance system" where it identifies and discards damaged or malfunctioning parts of a cell.

The term autophagy was first coined by Christian de Duve over 40 years ago, and is derived from Greek, and means "eating of self."[191]

In the simplest of terms, autophagy is a form of cellular maintenance or cleansing, and it is an extremely important first step in the process of replacing damaged components with newly built components within your body. Simply put, it is the cleanup that needs to happen before growth and repair can occur.

During any given day of our lives there are millions of cellular reactions that occur in our bodies, and overtime, some of these reactions can lead to damage—just like adding miles to a car eventually leads to wear and tear. Only unlike a car, our bodies have their own built in mechanics that can identify and repair this wear and tear, when given the opportunity to do so.

Interestingly, the lack of properly functioning autophagy is thought to be one of the main reasons for the accumulation of cellular damage within our bodies and thus accelerated aging within the human body. In other words, the process of autophagy may be an essential part of the anti-aging mechanism and one of the major health benefits of fasting.

The problem with autophagy is that the act of eating tends to get in its way. It seems that lab animals and human beings left to eat as they please do too little autophagic recycling. The resulting accumulation of damaged cellular machinery can cause a wide range of unhealthy effects, including the accumulation of damaged mitochondria, which increases the production of reactive oxygen species, accelerating further damage and possibly even the aging process by limiting the deposition of aggregate-prone proteins and the formation of damaging reactive oxygen species by mitochondria.[192] So the more time spent in the fed state, the less time you have to really ramp up the autophagic process within your body.

The strong connection between autophagy and fasting is due to the fact that the principle signal to turn up the autophagy dial is the act of entering the fasted state. And if fasting is the signal to turn on autophagy, then eating is the signal to turn it off. Even small amounts of glucose or amino acids are able to inhibit autophagy, as amino acids together with the hormone insulin are its principle negative regulators.[193]

And it doesn't take a feast to negatively affect autophagy. Recent research that was published in 2010 found a 3-gram dose of the branched chain amino acid leucine combined with 7 grams of EAA (10 grams of total amino acids) was enough to decrease autophagy markers in otherwise fasting humans.[194] So even a small meal in the middle of a fast may be enough to blunt the increased autophagic processes associated with fasting.

The upregulation of autophagy seems to be unique to the fasting state, as well as possibly the exercised state, and it can easily be undone by even a small ingestion of food, specifically protein and/or amino acids.

So how important is autophagy to your overall health?

Autophagy is of increasing interest as a target for cancer therapy,[195] treatment of alcoholic liver disease,[196] and as a crucial defense mechanism against malignancy, infection, and neurodegenerative disease.[197, 198, 199, 200, 201]

The research on fasting and neuronal diseases such as Huntington's and Alzheimer's is also beginning to look very promising as fasting has been found to cause a rapid and profound upregulation of autophagy in the brain,[202, 203, 204] which has the potential to remove toxic molecules and damaged mitochondria from neurons.[205, 206, 207, 208]

Research has even found that autophagy can help the body defend against both bacteria and viruses.[209, 210, 211, 212]

So the process of autophagy and its importance in cellular maintenance or cleansing is the main reason why some researchers are speculating that intermittent fasting can improve neuronal function and overall health in a way that is unique from any other style of dieting or calorie restriction.[213],[214]

It is also the reason why some people think that intermittent fasting can help regulate the aging process. Since "aging" refers to the biological changes that occur during a lifetime that result in reduced resistance to stress, increased vulnerability to disease, and an increased probability of death, autophagy can improve many of these areas.[215]

Finally, it's not just your health that benefits from autophagy promoted by fasting—optimal autophagic flux is required for the maintenance of the integrity of skeletal fibers, which are the basic contractile units of skeletal muscles.[216]

Both excess and reduced levels of autophagy are detrimental for muscle health; the former results in the loss of muscle mass, whereas the latter causes skeletal fiber degeneration and weakness.[217] So you wouldn't want autophagy on all the time, but you do need a healthy balance of autophagy and growth for the optimal functioning of the human body.

In fact, autophagy is actually necessary to maintain muscle mass, and inhibition/alteration of autophagy can contribute to myofibril degeneration (degeneration of individual muscle fiber) and weakness in muscle disorders characterized by accumulation of abnormal mitochondria and inclusions.[218]

Since autophagy helps cells break down defective components such as misshapen proteins and dysfunctional mitochondria, it is what ensures that your muscles are full of fully functional proteins, and not simply a conglomeration of damaged or malfunctioning proteins.

By allowing for growth when we eat, and the autophagic process of repair maintenance and cleansing when we are fasting, we help restore a balance in the body that may be a missing link in the prevention of many of today's deadly and debilitating diseases such as cancer, Alzheimer's and Huntington's disease, liver disease, and even loss of muscle size and function.

Health Benefits – The Conclusion

As you can see, fasting has been an often-overlooked answer to the health and weight management needs of many people. For the vast majority of us, the answer to the question, "Could we benefit from taking an occasional break from eating?" is a resounding, "YES"!

For healthy people wanting a simple and effective way to lose weight, the combination of short-term fasting and exercise is an easy way to create a caloric deficit without a negative impact on our metabolism or our muscle.

Not only is fasting an effective way to reduce our calorie intake, it also helps to restore a normal balance between fed and fasted metabolism. Far too many of us are spending every waking moment of our lives in the fed metabolism, under the misled "guidance" of today's health and nutrition recommendations.

This new balance helps reduce our body fat levels, as well as many markers of inflammation and disease risk. It can even upregulate the process of autophagy, potentially protecting from a whole host of diseases later in life, and allowing the body to perform needed maintenance and cleansing at the cellular level. Now, when it comes to many of the other astounding benefits that fasting is reported to have, the evidence is not as concrete, but it is still very promising.

Fasting, and even the act of simply eating less, has been found to have positive effects on lifespan, disease, and aging in research using animals (mostly mice).[219] However, recent research conducted by the National Institute on Aging has started to uncover that some of these health and longevity benefits occur in primates like monkeys, leading to speculation that fasting may have some similar benefits in humans.[220]

What is even more remarkable is that fasting has been shown to decrease many markers of risk of coronary artery disease, leading researchers to speculate that a lifestyle that includes short periods of fasting may decrease the risk of heart disease.[221]

When you consider all of these benefits including the possible benefits that fasting can have on inflammation, autophagy, and the possible risk of disease such as cancer, diabetes, and cardiovascular disease, it becomes clear that fasting for 24-hours once or twice per week, may be the easiest way to decrease your calorie intake by 10% to 20%, without having to sacrifice and restrict what you eat during the times when you are not fasting. It's like getting the benefits of an entire week of strict dieting, while only sacrificing for one or two days.

So, with fasting we can create prolonged dietary restriction (the only proven *nutritional* method of weight loss) while only sacrificing one or two 24-hour periods in a week, allowing us to reset the balance between fed and fasted. Using this method allows us to eat less, and reap the health benefits of fasting while still enjoying the foods we eat, since it does not limit the types of foods we eat, or the styles in which we eat them when we are not fasting.

The best part of these findings is that since many of the health benefits from fasting occur in the first 24-hours, we can use the *Eat Stop Eat* style of flexible intermittent fasting and **NEVER GO A DAY WITHOUT EATING!**

The Eat Stop Eat Way of Life

It is important to note right away that I do not consider this a diet program. There are no phases, no point systems, no weighing foods, and most importantly no foods that are ever off-limits.

I am not going to tell you that sugar is the cause of our obesity problem, because it's not—neither is fat. Part of the cause of our obesity problem is that we are failing to realize that we're looking for the answer in the wrong places.

Obesity is not created by one specific macronutrient in our diet. In fact, it's not the diet at all. In my opinion, the number one cause of our obesity epidemic is abundance. There simply is too much food available for us to consume. As I said earlier, each day in the United States, the food industry produces enough food to supply every single person with almost 4,000 calories (almost double what we typically need in a day).[222]

Combine this with a highly effective and relentless food marketing industry and a misled and backwards health and nutrition industry and the problem becomes clear.

Not only do most of us eat too much, but most of us have no idea why

This is why *Eat Stop Eat* is not a diet; it is a lifestyle based on the nutritional custom of including the combination of short-term, flexible, and intermittent fasting along with resistance training into your life.

It's a way of life where you accept the idea of taking small 24-hour breaks from eating, and taking part in resistance exercises (working out with weights) at least two to three times a week. That's it. The *Eat Stop Eat* lifestyle is simply taking a 24-hour break from eating once or twice per week and a commitment to a workout routine.

All my research has led me to the conclusion that this is the single best and most uncomplicated way to lose weight, to maintain muscle, and to reap all the amazing health bene-fits associated with fasting. Keep in mind, brief breaks from eating are nothing new — almost all of us fast for 8 to 10 hours almost every night, so I'm simply asking you to expand this fast. It is also the easiest way to rid you of obsessive-compulsive eating and the need to constantly scour magazines and the internet for the latest and greatest diet strategy.

With *Eat Stop Eat*, you get rid of the compulsion and guilt that drives so many of today's eating habits, as we get rid of the idea that you need to be constantly eating, or that there is even one true "perfect" way to eat. The reason I don't consider this style of eating to be a diet is because unlike almost all popular diets, the *Eat Stop Eat* lifestyle is a sustainable addition to the way we eat for the rest of our lives.

It is the easiest way to lose fat, feel fit, and maintain a lean body as it does not require any difficult nutritional planning. It does not require special shopping trips, exotic foods, or expensive supplements. It simply asks you to refrain from eating for one or two 24-hour periods every week.

It is the highly adaptable aspects of *Eat Stop Eat* that allow people to use it successfully to lose weight, and it's what allows them to keep the weight off for years afterwards. And don't worry if you can't fast for 24-hours every time. Twenty-four hours was chosen through my research simply because it was any easy time-frame to remember, allowed people to eat every day, and was suitable for all different levels of body fat and weight loss needs. That being said, there is still a benefit to fasting for 16 hours, or 20 hours. The point is, as long as you are fasting intermittently (while still eating every day) and resistance training while keeping your lifestyle flexible, you're doing *Eat Stop Eat*.

In fact, with *Eat Stop Eat* you are losing fat by doing nothing: not cooking, not eating, and not worrying about what you will eat when you're eating. In exchange, you spend a little time lifting weights (which you should be doing anyway for the health benefits of exercise itself) and trying to be somewhat responsible on the days that you are eating.

Best of all, with *Eat Stop Eat* style fasting, you never go a day without eating!

How to Fast Eat Stop Eat Style

In order to fast for 24 hours, you can simply eat as you normally would until 6:00 pm on day one, and then fast until 6:00 pm the following day. As an example, you could start your fast on Monday at 6:00 pm and finish your fast on Tuesday at 6:00 pm. People who follow *Eat Stop Eat* call this a dinner-to-dinner fast.

By fasting in this manner, you manage to eat every day; however you also manage to take a 24-hour break from eating. More importantly, you break the horrible habit of continuously being in the fed state, thereby resetting your metabolic balance between fed and fasted.

You can also adjust this to fit your own personal lifestyle. This is how you can make *Eat Stop Eat* work for you. If a dinner-to-dinner fast does not work for you, try my personal favorite time frame and go 2:00 p.m. to 2:00 p.m. instead (aptly called the lunch-to-lunch fast). Remember, the *Eat*

Stop Eat lifestyle is designed to be very flexible. The key is to make sure you are asleep during the parts of the fast that you find toughest. As an example, if you find the beginning of a fast harder than the end then you may want to try fasting from 8 p.m. to 8 p.m.

It is this flexibility that makes *Eat Stop Eat* so easy. If you were planning on starting your fast on Tuesday, but something came up and you had to go to dinner with friends on Tuesday night, there is no need to worry because you can simply start the fast the next day.

Also, keep in mind that as your life changes so should your fasts. A dinner-to-dinner fast may be perfect for you when you first start fasting, but after a couple months you may find yourself having a hard time finishing your fasts, or feeling a strong urge to overeat after you fast. The quickest and easiest solution is to try a different fast time. This slight change can have dramatic results on keeping your fasts both easy and effective. Always test new fast times before trying longer fasts. Remember, keeping it flexible is the key to long-term sustained weight loss.

Another important aspect of *Eat Stop Eat* style fasts is that you do drink during your fasts. During your fasts you may drink any calorie-free beverages you like.

As an example, these are all drinks that would be permissible during your fast:

- Black Coffee
- Black tea
- Green tea

- Herbal tea
- Water
- Sparkling water
- Even diet soda pop (if you are the type of person who drinks diet soda)

Keep in mind that a significant portion of your daily liquid intake comes from the water in the food you eat, and since you're not eating when your fasting, it is advisable to drink a little more than you normally would.

Try your best to keep your calories as close to zero as possible. Once you start adding a "little bit" of cream and sugar to your coffee, or a "little sip" here or there you may

find that your calorie intake slowly starts to creep up during your fast. Do your best to try and have a "zero tolerance approach" during your fast.

When it comes to what else you can eat during your fasts, follow this guideline—the true benefit is learning to take breaks from eating, not to figure out how to "game the system."

I often get questions about consuming a "little bit" of beef broth, or coconut water, or xylitol, or other almost calorie-free foods during a fast. There is not enough research for me to answer questions on the metabolic effect of a small amount of calories from all the different food and ingredient sources. So, remember that calorie-free beverages are okay during your fasts, and calorie-free gum is all right in moderation, but try to avoid any other almost calorie-free foods. The key is to learn to take a break from eating, not to continue to reinforce the pattern of always eating and always being fed.

So, when it comes to what you can and cannot eat while fasting, follow this simple guideline: *If you can go without then go without, but if you really can't go without then don't.*

If you are sick, or aren't feeling well, then you do not have to fast. If work gets hectic or you've increased your exercise volume so much that fasting isn't practical for a period of time, then again, don't fast. *Eat Stop Eat* is a flexible long-term solution. On some weeks you may fast once, others twice. It's all up to you and your personal preferences. Just do what works for you!

To start, try one fast per week. Experiment with what times work best for you. Once you have the hang of fasting then you can increase the amount of times per week that you fast.

Avoid the mistakes of trying to fit as many fasts into a week as possible, or trying to extend your fasts far beyond 24 hours. As I mentioned earlier, I have found that 24-hours once or twice a week is the most flexible and convenient way to fast.

Extending beyond this greatly reduces the flexibility of *Eat Stop Eat* and may lead to a sort of "fasting burnout." Forcing yourself to fast too often or for too long to the point where you are dreading your next fast completely defeats the purpose of the *Eat Stop Eat* lifestyle.

The same goes for fasting more often, as I'll discuss in the next couple of chapters—the benefits of fasting don't only come just from the time you are fasting, but also the time after the fast. Just like with exercise, there needs to be recovery time for you to get the full effects. That's why I rec-ommend at least 48-hours of time in between each 24-hour fast.

After talking with literally hundreds of people who have been following *Eat Stop Eat*, I have noticed that the people who stay flexible and relaxed see the best weight loss results and are the most able to keep the weight off. On the other hand, the people who try to speed up the process by fasting multiple times per week or extending their fasts to 48 or even 72-hours do see quick results, but also "burn out" very quickly.

This is in agreement with the large volume of research on restrained eating, which eloquently shows that the more restrained a person is with their eating, meaning the more rules they try and follow (good food/bad food lists, food combining, etc.) the more likely they will see quick weight loss, but also the more likely they will experience extreme weight rebounds after they have broken some of their rules and restraints.[223, 224]

Under similar conditions, the more restrained you are with your fasts, the more likely you will feel guilty if you break your rules and end up overeating.

The bottom line is that the *Eat Stop Eat* lifestyle should free you from obsessive-compulsive eating, but this should not be at the expense of simply learning to obsess about your fasting.

The same "fasting burnout" happens to people who combine fasting with strict dieting, or excessive amount of exercise. As a general rule of thumb, if you are having difficulties organizing fasting, exercising, and dieting into your schedule you are most likely doing too much of at least one of these activities.

I'd like you to perform weight training at least twice per week, and you can add in cardio-style training if you wish, just make sure you are adequately recovering from your workouts and fasts. With regards to dieting, as a general rule of thumb, if you are fasting, then on the days you are eating you should not be in any more than a 10% to 20% deficit for any length of time. Your once-or-twice-per-week fasts are meant to be a replacement for traditional dieting. If you have a significant amount of weight to lose then you may be able to handle both fasting and eating at a slight deficit, but the leaner you get, the less this is advised. Remember, the goal is not 0% body fat.

Consider fasting the easiest way possible to get results. Essentially you are getting results from doing nothing, so you do not need to make it any more complicated than an occasional break from eating, but you should go out of your way to view every single complete fast as a "mini-victory"—positive reinforcement at its finest.

Eat Stop Eat –
Why Not Longer Fasts?

There are reasons that I prefer 24-hour fasts over longer fasts. One is the ease and simplicity of 24-hour fasts; another is that they allow people to still eat every day. I also believe the goal should be to balance the times spent fed and fasted, rather than to completely remove eating for days on end.

To understand the main reason why I do not promote the idea of longer fasts I'm going to need to introduce you to the reciprocal relationship that exists in your body between your fat burning metabolism and your carbohydrate burning metabolism.

In order to meet the energy requirements of an average day, your body will burn a blend of carbohydrates and fats. In the resting state (not exercising), this blend will largely be determined by the blend of carbohydrates and fats in your diet.

As you gradually start to enter the fasted state, this blend will slowly favor fat over carbohydrates, and this is for good reason.

As I mentioned earlier, when you fast for short periods of time your blood sugar remains stable. It will drop from the high levels that you typically have after eating a meal, down to what we call fasted levels and then stay there. We have known this since 1855, when scientist Claude Bernard discovered that during the initial stages of fasting, the blood sugar level was kept normal due to the breakdown of the liver glycogen.[225]

Liver glycogen (the sugar being stored in your liver) is what keeps your blood sugar stable at normal levels while you are fasting for short periods of time. However, if you keep fasting eventually you liver glycogen will begin to run out, and other compensatory mechanisms must come in to play to maintain your blood sugar levels.

As you fast, you slowly enter fasted state metabolism—a metabolism based around mobilizing and using your body fat as a fuel. Fasted state metabolism is a fat-burning metabolism—using fat (and later ketones) as a fuel in order to preserve your blood sugar levels and your body protein stores. This is true during short 12 to 24-hour fasts and much longer fasts.

The longer you fast, the greater the alterations that must be made to ensure that you are able to burn as much fat as possible. In short, the longer your fast, the more fat burning dominates carbohydrate burning. Once you are this far into fat burning, you simply cannot turn it off like a switch when you start eating again. And this is where some of the scare about longer term fasting comes from.

Specifically, an increase in blood free fatty acid levels is well known to push your muscles towards oxidizing a high amount of fat as a fuel, but in doing so it must also inhibit glucose oxidation.[226] This change begins very early during a fast, as early as the 8 to 10-hour mark, and then gradually progresses as the level of free fatty acids build up in your blood and the level of glycogen decreases in your liver.

There is no real way around this. If you want your muscles to burn your body fat as a fuel, then you can't have your muscles also burn high amounts of carbohydrates. And since your muscles are not oxidizing carbohydrates, less glucose is actually entering your muscles. It's still in your blood, but your muscles don't want any. They are "full" from a carbo-hydrate point of view—there would be no place to put the glucose if it entered your muscles.

As a result, it is a well-established fact that longer periods of fasting (48 to 72-hours and beyond) not only induce a high level of fat oxidation, but also create a short period of insulin resistance at the muscular level in the immediate hours after the fast is finished.[227]

Now, this doesn't happen during a 24-hour fast as it takes around 24-hours just to deplete liver glycogen levels,[228] but once glycogen has been depleted and the levels of fat in your blood are increased, changes start to occur to ensure that your blood sugar levels still remain stable, even in the face of diminished glycogen stores. This seems to happen earlier in women than in men, possibly due to the fact that women have higher levels of fat in their blood and a better ability to burn fat while in the fasted state. Basically, women enter fasted state metabolism quicker than men.

So, when you fast for extended periods (two to three days and beyond) your body goes into a kind of permanent fat burning physiology which involves a down regulation of the hormones and enzymes responsible for carbohydrate burning.

Normally, this isn't an issue since during short fasts we start to enter the fasted state and increase the amount of fat we burn, but we begin eating again before the body can compensate for these maintained elevations in fat burning by decreasing insulin sensitivity.

However, when you greatly pass 24-hours of fasting by 2 to 3-fold, this decreased sensitivity to insulin can build up and carry over to when you are eating. Towards the end of longer-term fasts your body will release far more fat into your bloodstream than you can actually use without adding in some form of exercise. So, even though you've ended your fast and had a meal, it's not as if all of those FFA that were released from your body fat stores suddenly vanish—they need some time to either be burned as a fuel, or restored as body fat.

Now, if for some reason all of these changes were to immediately reverse after your first bite of a meal after your fast, you would experience some very nasty consequences. Firstly, you'd risk becoming hypoglycemic; you'd also have an extremely high fat level in your blood with no way to get rid of that fat, except to re-store it all immediately as body fat. Neither one of these are ideal situations and for these reasons it takes your body a period of time (several hours) to come back into a normal state with normal levels of insulin sensitivity after longer fasts.

In fact, fasting for 72-hours can temporarily blunt insulin's ability to prevent lipolysis[229, 230] even in the fed state. This illustrates the transition state that occurs after a longer fast. The elevated levels of growth hormone that are released into your blood following a longer-term fast does not vanish the minute you take a bite of your first meal, and can actually take several hours to come back down to non-fasting levels.

So just as you "ramp up" into fat burning mode in a fast, you also have to "ramp down" at the end of a fast.[231 232] However, it's also been found that after this acute period of insulin resistance your body may actually return to a level of improved insulin sensitivity—as periods of longer fasting are associated with improvements in insulin sensitivity when measured several days later.

The bottom line is that there is a major switch from glucose oxidation to fatty acid oxidation that occurs during fasting, and this switch needs some time to become apparent. What may be less obvious is that this switch requires a similar duration of time to be undone when refeeding commences. In other words, there is a gradual transition into fasted state metabolism and there is a gradual transition back into fed state metabolism. Finally, the longer the time spent in the fasted state, the longer it takes to return to the fed state.

In the end, I'm not sure how short periods of acute insulin resistance affect human health, some people have even argued that they are good for long-term health and anti-aging.[233, 234]

These are just some of the reasons why *Eat Stop Eat* is based around brief 24-hour periods of fasting. There is ease and flexibility associated with 24-hours of fasting divided between two days, but this ease and flexibility is erased when you begin to fast for longer periods of time.

The bottom line is that almost everyone can fast for 24-hours, but NOT everyone can do more. For that reason, 24-hours once or twice per week, separated by 2 to 6-days of normal, responsible eating and regular exercise is the *Eat Stop Eat* prescription for weight loss and overall health.

How to Eat, Eat Stop Eat Style

The point of *Eat Stop Eat* isn't to force you to not eat; it's actually to give you the freedom to eat. That's how balance works. If I could describe *Eat Stop Eat* without using the word "fasting" it would be, *"the freedom to choose when you eat, and also when you don't eat."*

During the times when you are eating, simply maintain the caloric intake that you **normally** eat while maintaining your bodyweight, while trying to obey what I like to call the "golden guideline of eating."

Eat less, while enjoying the foods you eat. Eat lots of fruits and vegetables, and lots of herbs and spices. And maybe most importantly, spend less time stressing over the types of food you are eating.

Pay special attention to that last sentence. All of the posturing and positioning by nutrition experts, and all of the scientists touting their research studies and their so-called conclusions are all based on the assumption that we need to be eating continuously every day. That's why the debate is always about "*what*" you should be eating, since the arguments are made under the assumption that no matter what, you will be eating something.

If you start living the *Eat Stop Eat* lifestyle, all of this becomes a moot point. You can reap the benefits of a low-calorie diet, and the benefits of short-term fasting, while eating in a way that is sustainable and enjoyable, just by adding one or two 24-hour fasts into your week.

With as little as two fasting periods added into your week, you can create the equivalent of a 20% reduction in calories. For a person eating 2,500 calories per day, that's the equivalent of reducing your calorie intake to 2,000 every day of the week! That's a 500 calorie drop, every day. A drop that is the equivalent of removing an entire cheeseburger with a side order of fries from your diet EVERY DAY!

Even a single fast a week can help create a small, yet sustainable 10% reduction in calories—the perfect option for people who are almost at their goal weight and simply do not need to, or want to fast twice in a single week.

The key to making *Eat Stop Eat* work for you is self-control. This is NOT a "fast once or twice a week and eat anything and everything you want every other day" type of lifestyle. Fasting may have a myriad of health benefits, but it is NOT magic.

Eat Stop Eat is NOT a feast-and-fast approach to healthy eating. It is a lifestyle that interrupts periods of normal maintenance-level eating with a 24-hour break. I think this is a fair trade. While most diet programs ask you to give up certain foods or entire food groups, all I am asking of you is to keep eating the way you normally eat—however, please try to eat sensibly and responsibly.

For some people eating sensibly and responsibly may be a departure from how you normally eat, and there may need to be some adjustments made to how you eat in between your fasts. This is especially true if the way you have been eating has been causing you to gain large amounts of weight. But in general, I'd like you to approach these periods as weight maintenance as opposed to being periods of more dieting.

After you have completed your fast, it is important that you go back to eating as you normally would to maintain your weight. Pretend that the fast never happened. Remind yourself that you do not need to reward yourself with extra-large helpings or extra desserts. Also remind yourself that you just created a large caloric deficit, so there is no need to starve yourself between your fasts. You also do not need any special post-fast rituals or supplements in order to make your fasting effective. Just resume eating as you would have on any other normal day. The purpose of the fast is to add small breaks to your *normal eating routine*.

As soon as you start coming up with special ways to eat and things to do at the end of your fast you're complicating things and missing the point of the simplicity of *Eat Stop Eat*. You are also missing the simplicity of *Eat Stop Eat* if you attempt to stack fasting on top of chronic dieting. Remember, *Eat Stop Eat* was meant to be a replacement for long-term diets, not an addition to them.

If you want to improve your nutrition while living the *Eat Stop Eat* lifestyle, go ahead. Nothing but good things will happen if you incorporate a little more fruits and vegetables into your diet and cut back on the sugar, but do whatever is within your own personal comfort zone. I believe the biggest health benefits will come from the fast, but all positive changes will help.

If you are following my one simple guideline (from the previous page) you will find that you are already making strides to eating a better diet.

I could spend pages telling you about the importance of eating real food over food-like substances, but if you are eating lots of fruits and vegetables then you are probably already doing this.

I could also tell you about the benefits of avoiding over-flavoring your food with salt and sugar, but if you are eating lots of herbs and spices you are already doing this too.

Finally, I could tell you about avoiding overly processed foods but if you are both eating less and eating more fruits and vegetables, then you are already accomplishing this.

While you may find this guideline overly simplistic at first, the truth is there is NO "normal" or "perfect" way to eat for weight loss. This is the great fallacy behind most diet books. The fact is, and always will be, it is calorie restriction that causes weight loss. And, properly balancing calorie restriction with the demands of your life allows that weight loss to be long-term weight loss.

Any diet book or diet style that claims they have the secret answer or that their way is the "only way that works" is

INSTANTLY proven wrong by the millions of people who have successfully lost weight by using alternative methods.

For instance, if I were to say that the *Eat Stop Eat* style of fasting is the ONLY way to lose weight I would INSTANTLY lose all credibility since it is entirely possible to lose weight without following the *Eat Stop Eat* style of fasting (it just wouldn't be as easy).

The point I am trying to make is that there is NO such thing as an all-encompassing way to define eating "normal." Humans can adapt to a wide variety of feeding regimens depending on their habitual meal patterns. In other words, eating "normal" is simply whatever you happen to be used to doing.

This is why I don't ever attempt to define "normal eating" or a "normal diet." What is a normal diet to someone who lives in Cairo, Egypt would be very abnormal to someone who lives in Pittsburgh, USA; while the diet of someone who lives in Pittsburgh, USA would not seem normal to someone who lives in Bridgetown, Barbados.

Your ancestry, your geography, how you were raised, your personal preferences, as well as your personal goals, define what normal is to you. You simply cannot define it in one way for everyone in the world. And, you certainly cannot let someone else define it for you.

People eat different types of food in different countries around the world. The way or style in which they eat is also different. Some countries have their meals at very specific times, whereas in other countries people eat at any time.

In Nepal, a typical family does not have breakfast. They have tea around 6 or 7 in the morning, and then they have their lunch from 9 to 10 in the morning. Supper would be around 8 or 9 in the evening.

In Spain, eating hours are also very different. In Madrid, you can eat at any time, though lunch is typically at 2 in the afternoon and dinner is at 9 or 10 at night. In Portugal lunch is typically at around 1 in the afternoon and dinner is typically at 8 in the evening or later.

In North America, we eat whenever possible. We eat standing up, walking to an appointment, in a meeting, in a hallway, on the subway, in the car, even while lying in bed. We eat wherever it's convenient and even wherever it is not convenient. We eat while watching movies at a movie theater and can even have an ice-cream sandwich during the intermission of a Broadway play.

Even the "traditional" breakfast, lunch, and dinner are only a recent phenomenon that may mean different things to different cultures.

Judging from early cookbooks and historical dietary literature breakfast was very rare, and was only recommended for children, invalids, and the elderly who have weak digestive systems.

The word "dinner" actually comes from the Latin "disjejunare," meaning "to un-fast" or break the fast of the evening. Remarkably, the word was contracted in the Romance languages to "disnare" or "disner" in Old French, or dinner in English. Thus, the word dinner actually means "breakfast."

Finally, lunch as a meal is a relatively new phenomenon.

Dr. Johnson's Dictionary (1755) said "lunch" or "luncheon" was, "As much food as one's hand can hold."[235] By the early nineteenth century, lunch had become a sit-down meal at the dining table in the middle of the day. By the late nineteenth century, luncheon had become a social occasion mainly for elite women.[236]

Nowadays, lunch has turned into a mid-day feast that can consist of a foot-long sandwich stacked with extra meat and cheese (served in a combo with a large soda and a bag of chips)!

Depending on where you live and your family customs, your eating habits could be very different from your neighbors or from what is being recommended in today's health and fitness magazines. This doesn't make them wrong, it just makes them different.

As you can see there is no such thing as eating normally which makes it impossible to define it. And, pushing yourself to eat in predetermined way with high amount of restraint and forbidden foods can actually worsen your chances of losing weight. This is why I suggest "eating responsibly" over dieting. Eating responsibly is much easier to define. Simply put, eating responsibly is eating the AMOUNT of food necessary to reach your bodyweight goal, while doing your best to make smart food choices that include a lot of variety.

Eating responsibly is also a mindset. It is realizing that on many occasions you are going to want to eat more food than you need to. If your goal is to lose weight, then eating responsibly means recognizing when you are eating too much and either, A) making the decision to stop eating, or B) accepting the fact that at that time you are going to eat more and you will deal with the results later.

There is no free pass to weight loss. Or, as science fiction writer Robert Heinlein would say, "There ain't no such thing as a free lunch."

And, despite what some people like to preach, you simply cannot eat as much as you want and still lose weight as long as you take supplement X or follow diet Y or exercise routine Z.

Even getting the fat cut right off your body in a surgical procedure *still* does not constitute permanent weight loss. (Yes, you can eat enough food to put that weight right back on! The remaining fat cells can still expand and fill up with fat if you continue to wolf back massive amounts of calories after the surgery.)

Finally, it is the last part of my guideline that could very well be **the most important part:**

> *Eat less, while enjoying the foods you eat. Eat lots of fruits and vegetables, and lots of herbs and spices. And maybe most importantly,* **spend less time stressing over the types of food you are eating.**

This is the very important (and VERY underrated) goal of having a good healthy relationship with the foods you eat. I know this sounds very "new age" but I assure you that a lot of today's overeating and obsessive compulsive eating habits come from unhealthy relationships with food, where people feel stressed and guilty every single time they eat. If you are enjoying the foods you eat, and not stressing about your food choices, then you are doing an amazing job avoiding this problem.

So with the *Eat Stop Eat* lifestyle (where rational simplicity is always the goal), this one simple guideline is all you need to guide your eating habits. However, if you would like to try and improve how you eat for the purpose of overall health, there are steps you can take.

When it comes to health, I simply do not agree with the common suggestion that the secret to eating for health is avoidance, yet this is where 99.99% of all of our nutrition recommendations come from.

For example, you may have read some or all of the following items to avoid: "At all costs avoid caffeine, sugar, white potatoes, saturated fat, trans fats, artificial sweeteners, artificial colors, artificial flavors, bread, gluten, legumes, dairy, anything cooked, and non-organic foods."

I'm sure you've read this type of nutrition advice before. In my opinion, this is a form of scaremongering. In fact, I'd go so far as to say it is dietary extremism masquerading as healthy eating, and it can actually damage your chances of losing weight.

Attempting to adhere to a very strict diet with large lists of foods you are not allowed to eat typically ends up in failure, due to something called the "disinhibition effect"—a paradox where merely labeling certain types of food as "off limits" or "forbidden" creates a disinhibition; where eating the foods you consider forbidden leads to increased eating afterwards.[237]

This disinhibition is not a result of the specific type of food, or its calorie content[238] or even its macronutrient profile.[239] Rather, it comes from the self-created belief that certain foods are forbidden, and the feeling of failure you get after eating them.

Indeed, the very act of eating even a small amount of a "forbidden" food can cause a person enough stress and anxiety that they actually overeat even more afterwards.

This is the opposite of what happens to a flexible dieter, who while still reducing overall calories does not follow an all-or-none approach to restraining the types of foods they can eat. Flexible dieters do not suffer from disinhibition effect, and if they eat a small amount of dessert they do not feel the need to overindulge afterwards, probably because they do not feel like they "blew it."[240]

So, following these "good food, bad food" type of diets can actually worsen your chances of maintaining long-term weight loss. This has been illustrated in a very large body of research spanning over two decades, yet is somehow conveniently ignored by most diet experts.

If I had to pick one word to describe healthy eating it would be "variety." As much variety as you can fit into your life. There are hundreds, if not thousands of undiscovered chemicals in the foods we eat. From strawberries to steak, we have only a small understanding of the complexities of our foods. Many of these chemicals are inert (meaning neither good nor bad for us), however some will be good, and some may be bad. The way to balance all of this is with variety, by picking as many foods as possible. By striving to eat with variety we avoid overeating or undereating any one nutrient, discovered or yet to be discovered.

As an example, you do not need to avoid simple sugars in your diet. If you increase the variety of foods you eat, it becomes very difficult to over-eat any one type of food—whether it be sugar, fat, protein, salt, or anything else you'd care to name.

Even foods we have been led to believe are extremely healthy fail in comparison to variety.

A breakfast of raw cashews, organic yogurt, and coconut flakes followed by a cup of matcha green tea may sound extremely healthy, but without variety it becomes extremely limited. In fact, a person who eats this type of breakfast every day for months on end would probably benefit greatly from the occasional breakfast of eggs and bacon, or oatmeal and blueberries... just something DIFFERENT.

There is one problem with the concept of variety and that is that research has shown us that eating for variety tends to lead us to eating more.[241]

This is where self-control comes in. Just like the balance between fed/fasted and insulin/growth hormone, you also need to find a balance between eating for variety while still eating less so that you can lose weight.

This is another benefit of *Eat Stop Eat*. It allows you to eat less, without imposing any rules or restrictions that may limit your ability to eat for variety.

Living the *Eat Stop Eat* lifestyle is the simplest way to improve your health, without massively restricting the foods you are allowed to eat. This gives you your best chance to eat a wide variety of foods while still eating less, thus ensuring what I would consider to be an optimal approach to health and weight loss.

Here's another amazing benefit of the *Eat Stop Eat* lifestyle; research has shown that even if you were to gorge yourself on your eating days (which I do not recommend) to the point where you don't lose any weight at all, you will still see some of the health benefits associated with fasting, such as improved insulin sensitivity and decreased oxidant stress.[242]

Eating with variety and eating less without practicing restrained eating is a large part of the *Eat Stop Eat* lifestyle. Combined with the small wins you get every time you complete a 24-hour fast, you create a flexible and positive approach to eating and weight loss. And remember, *Eat Stop Eat* was meant to be an occasional break from your normal eating patterns. It was not meant to be a reason to fast every day, or as a reason to allow you to binge or feast after a fast. It is most effective when you approach it as a simple, yet powerful, way to eat a little less.

Finally, when it comes to eating—no one eats perfectly because perfect eating does not exist. There is no perfect diet or perfect food. At one time or another everyone eats treats and desserts. Everyone. The difference is that some feel guilty and ashamed, and some do not. So, don't feel like you need to eat perfectly, instead aim to eat in a way that suits you while allowing you maintain your weight while enjoying the foods you eat.

What to Do While Fasting

Since I do not consider the *Eat Stop Eat* lifestyle to be a diet, it would be a waste for me to fill two hundred pages of this book with recipes, food combining instructions or calorie and protein charts (go browse through any other diet book and you'll quickly discover that most of the pages are just that).

Doing so would not help you in any extra capacity. In fact, it would do quite the opposite. It would clutter your mind with needless rules to obsess and stress over, and possibly set you up for disinhibition effect while not moving you any closer to your weight loss goals. Instead, the best thing I can do is provide you some tips to help make your fasts a little easier.

The first and most important thing you need to remember is to drink a lot of calorie-free fluids; this will help you avoid getting thirsty, which is often mistaken as hunger.

In the morning start your day with a large glass of water. Black coffee and tea are also allowed during a fast. You may also find diet colas useful, and don't worry about having a small amount of artificial sweeteners during your fast, in my opinion the health benefits of fasting far outweigh any worry about the small and infrequent intake of artificial sweeteners.

Also, the current buzz about aspartame causing giant insulin spikes is not founded in science. There have been multiple studies on aspartame and its effect on insulin and growth hormone and they have all found no negative effects on either hormone.[243, 244]

My personal opinion is that you're not missing out on anything by avoiding aspartame, so when possible and within reason, make non-artificially-sweetened choices (especially when you are not fasting); however, I do not see them as being detrimental to your fasting.

The other common misconception about coffee, teas, and colas is that caffeine causes giant increases in insulin. While it is true that caffeine can cause an increased insulin response to large doses of carbohydrates (caffeine + carbs = more insulin release than carbs alone),[245, 246] I have never seen any research suggesting that caffeine alone, without any carbs, causes insulin release. From a metabolic point of view, these drinks should not interfere with your fasts. This being said, try to keep your coffee and tea consumption to roughly what it would be on the days you are not fasting. Remember fasting should not be an excuse to drastically alter how you eat or drink.

You may also find it helpful to stay busy while fasting. Recently I had someone tell me that, "Fasting is easiest when

I'm busy, I think if people's lives were a little more exciting they wouldn't need to eat so much to get some joy out of their day." This statement is very true.

Food is a form of bio-feedback. It is a form of stimulus in our everyday lives. So, when parts of our days are lacking excitement or stimulation (like when we are sitting in a car stuck in rush hour traffic), we seek stimulation in the form of foods and snacks.

Have you ever had a really boring day at work? Did you ever notice how often you snacked, or made coffee? This is because you are replacing mental stimulation with food stimulation.

A little complex, but it is the short answer to why we should stay busy while fasting. Other than staying busy, you can go about your day as if it were any other day. You can go to work, go shopping, go work out. Whatever it is you normally do during your day.

This is the beauty of the *Eat Stop Eat* lifestyle. It is the simplest way to lose fat and improve your health and well-being, without drastically changing the way you live.

In fact, you will probably find that you have a lot of spare time on your fasting day. Almost everyone who lives the *Eat Stop Eat* lifestyle experiences this new freedom and extra time. At this moment, you will also realize how much of your daily routine is spent planning, preparing, going out for, and eating food.

Taking a break from eating might just be the only way to actually free up useful time in your week.

Lastly, view every single fast you complete as a small win towards your weight loss goals. This is a unique feature that sets fasting apart from traditional dieting. By viewing each fast as a small win, you create a positive reinforcement as you move towards your weight loss goals. By conquering a fast you teach yourself that weight loss is possible, and that YOU are in control.

The main problem with traditional diets is that they seem like a long, slow march towards an inevitable failure. For example, going weeks and weeks without messing up or cheating only to hit that one day where you break and eat a donut. This only teaches you that you will inevitably fail at dieting; this negative reinforcement can destroy your future weight loss goals.

Stay positive and flexible with fasting. Every single 24-hour fast you complete is small win towards hitting your weight loss goals.

Fasting and Women (Special Considerations)

It should come as no surprise that there are obvious gender differences in how the human body works. From the way they look to their own unique metabolisms, men and women do have very different physiologies. In fact, there are entire books dedicated to the topic (my favorite being *Gender Differences in Metabolism* by Dr. Mark Tarnopolsky).

In short, aside from the differences in muscle mass and body fat levels, men and women also differ due to women having their own set of unique metabolic and physiologic needs that relate to their child-bearing physiology, and this fact simply cannot be ignored when discussing diet and weight loss.

In general, when comparing men and women, women tend to burn more fat on a day-to-day basis and are more insulin sensitive than men. Women also have very different hormonal profiles. There are the obvious differences in sex hormones like testosterone and estrogen which affect not only our ability to burn fat and build muscle, but also influence where we store our body fat.

There are also large differences in some of the more important fat loss hormones. Men tend to have less circulating growth hormone than women, and women tend to have 2 to 3-times more leptin than men.[247] A man's hormone levels also tend to be more stable than a woman's since many hormones tend to fluctuate within a women's menstrual cycle.[248]

The fact that both leptin and growth hormone are higher in women may have to do with the higher estrogen levels found in women's bodies. It has been shown in healthy pre-menopausal and post-menopausal women that estrogen increases blood GH levels.[249, 250] In fact, the combination of high estrogen and high growth hormone is one of the hallmark hormonal markers of healthy young women. A healthy, young woman may secrete anywhere from 2 to 7-fold more GH than pre-pubertal girls, men, or post-menopausal women.[251, 252, 253, 254]

Because of these hormonal differences women will have higher amounts of free fatty acids in their blood compared to a man after longer periods of fasting (40 to 72-hours). These elevated levels of free fatty acids will cause a woman to remain in a heightened state of fat burning longer than a man for the period after the fast has been broken. This is evident by the increased fat oxidation even after a meal, slower glucose clearance, and the decreased ability for elevated insulin to push a woman out of fat burning during the hours following a fast.[255]

So, it is true that women have a physiology that is uniquely their own, and many of these differences involve some of the most important fat-burning hormones. But how does this affect their ability to diet and lose unwanted body fat?

It is well known that prolonged food deprivation, large energy deficits created through vigorous exercise, and rapid weight loss all may result in various forms of menstrual dysfunction in some (but not all) women.[256, 257] This is often seen in women who are dieting for long periods of time as well as in female athletes who are not purposefully dieting, but unable to meet the caloric needs of their rigorous athletic regimen.

However, it's not just prolonged periods of time in large calorie deficits that are the problem but having too little fat may be a problem for some women in and of itself. In 1974, Frisch and McArthur theorized that the maintenance of normal menstrual function was related to a critical level of 22% body fat.[258] And, while the "healthy" amount of body fat is more likely a range than it is a hard, fast number like 22%; the fact remains, and bears repeating, that the goal of any diet program is not to obtain 0% body fat (I know this is obvious, but it needs to be stated loudly and often).

Or put differently, regardless of whether you are a man or a woman, young or old, bad things start to happen when your body fat levels become too low.

For men, the critical level of body fat seems to be closer to 4-6%,[259] but this also seems to vary slightly based on age and ethnicity. So, both men and women have healthy levels of body fat under which metabolic/hormonal issues may arise, with the levels for men being less than half that of women.

Research on elite national level female athletes has shown that the combination of low body fat levels with a large calorie deficit can result in amenorrhea (absence of their monthly period), as well as decreased leptin and estradiol levels.[260]

In this study, 39 national level female athletes were examined. The leanest women tended to be the ones who were amenorrhoeic, had the lowest levels of insulin, leptin, and estradiol. These women were roughly 23 years old, had a BMI of approximately 18 with a body fat level of around 15%. As an example, a 5'6" woman in this study would weigh around 112 pounds, burn almost 1,000 calories per day through exercise, while eating around 1,700 calories per day and only 55 grams of protein per day.

The women who still had normal menstrual cycles had slightly more body fat (15.5%), the same amount of lean mass, but ate almost 500 more calories a day, and significantly more protein (78 versus 55 grams per day). They also had higher levels of leptin, insulin, thyroid hormones, and leptin than their amenorrhoeic counterparts.

Even though these women were not fasting, this study shows that minimal levels of body fat, combined with long-term calorie deficits, and possible mild protein malnutrition can result in marked hormonal disruptions.

Based on these findings research has clearly shown that there are metabolic and physiologic differences between men and women in terms of their hormonal levels, their body fat levels and their response to dieting, however the idea that either men or women somehow cannot take an occasional break from eating is a fallacy. Both genders are equally suited to reap the health rewards of fasting, and each has their own unique problems they may encounter when they fast for too long or too often.

In general, women seem to be more protected against the stresses of 72-hour fasting than men. When men and women were fasted for 4 days straight, both sexes saw a decrease in levels of the active form of thyroid hormone (T3), however the fall was significantly greater in the men compared to the women. This difference was not related to body weight or to amount of weight loss during fasting and instead seemed to be due to the unique hormonal differences between men and women.[261]

Women also seem to improve their insulin sensitivity better than men during short periods of fasting (12 to 38 hours),[262, 263, 264] but their insulin sensitivity tends to worsen for a short period of time after longer fasts (48 to 72 hours) due to the high level of fat burning and free fatty acids being present in their blood in the hours after the fast.[265]

When men and women undergo prolonged periods of low-calorie intake, men see a significant decrease in testosterone levels. Women's testosterone, while much lower than men's, remains unchanged.[266]

Women release more of their body fat into their blood than men do during fasting, and although this seems obvious due to the fact that women typically carry more fat than men, research has shown that even when women and men are matched for their fat mass, women still release more fat during a fast than men.[267, 268] Women also have more fat-burning enzymes then men,[269] and thus an increased capacity to burn their body fat as a fuel.

Men and women are both able to increase the amount of fat released from their body fat stores and upregulate fat burning during a fast, however a women's increased ability to release body fat to be used as a fuel, increased levels of growth hormone, and a decreased susceptibility to metabolic disturbances seems to make them particularly well suited to using short-periods of fasting as a way to help them lose body fat.

Women lose fat, and the bad visceral fat, when they undertake various forms of intermittent fasting. They also see improvements in many markers of health, including cholesterol levels, triglyceride levels, and insulin sensitivity.[270, 271]

The one caveat to this statement would be women who are already very lean, or women who are extremely active.

To examine the effect of fasting on very lean women, 8 healthy, lean women with a BMI of 20 or less and a body fat percentage of 20 or less were asked to fast for 72-hours during the mid-follicular phase of their menstrual cycle (an important time in follicle development).

A typical woman in this study would be 28 years old, 5'6" tall and weigh 120 pounds, with 19% body fat. Keep in mind that many online body transformation contest winners end their transformations at around 18% body-fat[272] and according to the American Council on Exercise the minimal essential levels of body fat for women is suggested to be around 12%,[273] so these women were already very lean.

All of the women were active, but none of them exercised more than 1.5-hours at a time or more than 5 times in a week during the study period (which I should point out, is a very high amount of exercise per week by most standards). The reported physical activities included walking, weight lifting, aerobic dancing, and bicycling. In-line with the suggestions that total body fat is an important marker in women's health, the researchers noted that it was very difficult to find 8 women of this leanness with normal menstrual cycles.

During the 72-hour fast there was a large, almost 5-pound weight loss, reducing the weight of our 5'6" women down to around 115 pounds and dropping their BMI down to between 18-19.

Accompanying this weight loss were progressive changes in their reproductive hormones. The women saw increased levels of cortisol, and delayed follicular development. One of the women also became amenorrhoeic during the study period.[274]

These results are in direct contrast to the results that the same researchers found in a group of women who were around 25% body fat.[275] In this study, 12 women within 15% of their ideal body weight were studied during 72-hours of fasting hours during the mid-follicular phase of their menstrual cycle (the same phase as the lean women).

In this study follicle development, as assessed by daily ultrasound examination and estradiol measurements, was similar in all cycles and was followed by ovulation in all women; follicular and luteal phase lengths of fasted and fed cycles were also similar. So in the normal weight women, fasting for 72-hours seemed to have little effect on reproductive physiology.

This research suggests that lean women (towards the lower end of a "healthy BMI") may be at higher risk of developing neuroendocrine and follicular phase reproductive abnormalities when nutrition is completely withdrawn for 72 hours.

The bottom line is that 72 hours of fasting maybe too long for women who are already exceptionally lean and active.

While this may seem like a gender difference, it may not actually be specific to women. Men also experience significant decreases in testosterone after 72 hours of fasting.[276]

And after long periods of caloric restriction combined with near minimal levels of body fat, men can see large decreases in their testosterone.[277] So the reproductive effects of longer fasts happen in both men and women, but tend to go more noticed in women.

While the symptoms may manifest differently, longer fasts can have negative effects in both lean men and women. Fasting combined with excessive exercise and excessive dieting may also present typical overuse symptoms in both men and women including exhaustion and a tendency to binge eat.

Another unique trait of women is their monthly fluctuations in estrogen levels. These fluctuations may warrant consideration when dealing with both fasting and dieting as evidence from both human and animal studies indicate that food intake fluctuates during the menstrual cycle; it is lower in the periovulatory phase and greater in the early follicular and luteal phases.[278, 279, 280]

Since estrogen is known to depress appetite by decreasing sensitivity to food cues, there may be periods of a month were women find fasting and dieting harder or easier, depending on their natural hormonal fluctuations.[281]

So, while there are definite recognizable differences in how men and women respond to dieting and fasting I have seen no evidence to suggest that either men or women should not fast.

This is not to say that either sex can haphazardly use as much fasting as often as they like in an attempt to lose weight. In fact, it's quite the opposite. This is more evidence that if fasting is to be used on a regular basis as a method of weight control then it must be done with some common sense.

24 hours of fasting is enough to see impressive weight loss in both men and women, and while the temptation is there to simply continue fasting for longer periods of time, this may be accompanied by unwanted affects. As the old saying goes—there is such thing as too much of a good thing. When it comes to adding fasting to a diet and exercise program, remember that fasting is meant as a *replacement* for traditional dieting and excessive exercise for the purpose of weight loss. It was NOT meant to be an addition to it.

For the vast majority of men and women, fasting once or twice a week for 24 hours combined with an exercise program and sensible eating is enough to cause significant weight loss, and maintenance of that weight loss. Adding in longer fasts, fasting more often, or excessively dieting on the days you are not fasting may not necessarily bring the results you think, or hope, it will.

Just like exercise or dieting, fasting can be overdone. For both men and women, the best advice I can give is to fit your fasting into your life, allow fat loss to happen at a natural pace (don't try to force it by combining fasting, dieting, and excessive exercise), and remember that the goal is NOT 0% body fat (neither for men nor for women).

How to Work Out with Eat Stop Eat

Resistance training is an essential part of the *Eat Stop Eat* lifestyle. The combination of fasting and responsible eating will allow you to lose body fat quickly and easily, but it is your resistance-training workouts that will ensure you maintain (or even increase) the size of your muscles while you are losing body fat.

I think just about everyone will agree that working out with weights (or any other form of resistance) will result in increased muscle mass, given that the weight used is high enough and rest and recovery periods are adequate.

It was more than 30 years ago that a group of scientists proved that the amount you use your muscles is the main factor in influencing how big they are (other than genetics and height). In other words, while your genetics determine your overall muscle building potential, how much and how often you stress your muscles dictates how close you get to reaching that potential.[282]

Weight training while following the *Eat Stop Eat* lifestyle will work your muscles in a way that promotes growth and preserves muscle mass while you are losing body fat.

There are many other reasons that people follow resistance training programs, such as: to improve their skills at a sport (sport-specific training), to increase their strength (power lifting or Olympic lifting), the prevention of osteoporosis (loss of bone mass), or even as a form of rehabilitation from an injury.

All of these purposes represent effective uses of weight training, but for the purpose of *Eat Stop Eat*, we will concentrate on the use of weight training for the purpose of preserving muscle mass (and metabolic rate) while following a reduced-calorie diet. Of course, in doing so we reap all the other health benefits of resistance training including improved cholesterol levels, improved blood sugar control, increased bone density, improved insulin sensitivity, and the often underappreciated value of its ability to elevate mood, and improve body image (an invaluable part of any weight loss program).[283, 284]

There are many different types of resistance training workouts that complement the *Eat Stop Eat* lifestyle, and it is important to note that I am not an exercise physiologist. Even though I have spent over seven years working in the bodybuilding industry, and have obtained certification as a strength and conditioning specialist from the National

Strength and Conditioning Association, I do not consider myself an expert in this field.

So while I am not an expert in workout design, I can share with you the principles of resistance training that have been tested in scientific studies. If you are looking for a specific workout plan or blueprint, I highly recommend you seek the advice of an exercise physiologist (with at least a graduate level education) for a detailed and progressive workout program that fits your own personal goals and needs.

I often like to think of the legend of Milo of Croton when determining what will—and what will not—work as an effective workout program. Milo (sometimes referred to as Milos) was a six-time Olympic champion wrestler in the sixth century BC who used a rather unique training style to build his physique. Legend has it that Milo would lift a baby cow over his head every day until it became a full-grown cow. And, while this legend changes from Milo simply lifting the cow to Milo doing laps around the Pantheon while carrying the cow, the simple point is that this must have been an impressive feat of strength considering a full-grown cow can weigh as much as 1,000 pounds!

We can learn two important lessons from the legend of Milo. First, your workouts need to be progressive if you want to gain or even keep your muscle mass. In other words, as you grow stronger you must continue to increase the amount of work you do with your muscles.

In Milo's case, this was conveniently taken care of for him as the baby calf he began lifting slowly grew in size and weight with each passing day. The load that he lifted increased every single day—this is a perfect example of progressive overload.

You probably won't be lifting a baby cow as part of your workout routine, so in a more practical example you have three realistic ways that you can increase the amount of work your muscles do in a workout:

- Use more weight for a given exercise (intensity or stress)
- Lift the same weight more times (volume)
- Lift the same amount of weight more often throughout the week/month (frequency)

Typically, most weight training workouts that have been used in scientific studies use a combination of these three principles to ensure the workouts are progressive in nature.

Here is a simple example using the bicep curl exercise: Our baseline workout for bicep curls will be 1 set x 20 pounds x 10 repetitions, once per week. In this example, the total work for this exercise is 1 set of exercises using 20 pounds x 10 reps = 200 pounds of total work per week.

Let's look at three examples of how to change this total work, using intensity, volume, and frequency over the course of one week.

Intensity (or Stress)

You can increase the total work number from our example above by simply adding 5 pounds per repetition. The new equation would be **25 pounds** x 10 reps done once per week = 250 pounds of total work per week.

Volume

You can also increase the total work number by adding more reps per set. If we add 5 repetitions per set the new equation would be 20 pounds x **15 reps** done once per week = 300 pounds total work per week. Similarly, you can keep the reps the same but add an extra set. The equation would now be 20 pounds x 10 reps x **2 sets** = 400 pounds total work per week.

Frequency

Finally, you can increase the total work by adding more workouts per week. If you simply did our example workout twice in the same week the new total work equation would look like this: 20 pounds x 10 reps x **2 workouts** = 400 pounds total work per week.

By using any combination of increasing intensity, volume, or frequency you can ensure that your workouts remain progressive.

The second (and probably most important) lesson to be learned from Milo of Croton is that the exact details of what equipment and program you use and how you use them probably does not matter too much as long as you are sufficiently stressing your muscles. The resistance can come from your body weight, free weights (such as dumbbells), elasticized bands, machines, or even lengths of chain!

If there is any secret to weight training it is simply that consistency, effort, and proper recovery are what will get you the best results, and while there are many different ways you can perform a weight training workout, science has not yet identified the "best" way to work out and probably never will. However, scientific research can provide us with a rough but effective outline that we can use to determine the effectiveness of a workout program.

According to the scientific review entitled, "The Influence of Frequency, Intensity, Volume and Mode of Strength Training on Whole Muscle Cross-Sectional Area in Humans," muscles will increase in size when they are exercised within a range of two to four times per week, allowing enough time between workouts for proper recovery.[285] The amount of recovery time needed depends on your current training status and the stress of your previous workout. In other words, how accustomed you are to the workout and level of difficulty of the workout.

An optimal workout schedule should allow each major muscle group to be exercised roughly twice per week, which scientific research suggests is a sufficient amount for causing muscle growth and the preservation of muscle while you are dieting.

Exercise sessions should consist of between three and eight sets per muscle group (depending on the size of the muscle), with optimal results occurring when each major muscle group goes through 40-60 repetitions per workout. Examples of this style of workout would include any combination of sets and repetitions that allow a muscle to fatigue between the 6th and 15th-repetition.

There are many different ways a workout can be designed to meet these recommendations. Examples include 3 sets of

15 reps, 4 sets of 10 reps, 8 sets of 8 reps, or even 10 sets of 6 reps.

Hopefully, you can see that outside of these basic recommendations there are many different ways you can design a workout to meet your requirements, and I encourage you to try many different styles.

Truthfully, the general beliefs in this area are as muddled and confusing as they are in the field of nutrition. As an example, research has suggested that using a light weight for a high amount of reps (between 20-25) may be as efficient at building muscle as using heavy weights for low reps (between 1-5) as long as the total amount of work complete is equal.[286]

While obviously we still have a lot to learn when it comes to all of the mechanisms behind muscle growth, these guidelines are a good representation of what has been found to be effective in well-controlled clinical research.

The important thing to remember is that exercise serves a number of benefits. Besides simply building muscle, the effect of exercise on mood, self-esteem, and body image cannot be stressed enough. After all, what good is losing weight if you still don't feel good about yourself?

Designing Your Own Workout Program

In most research trials where people on a low-calorie diet preserved lean mass by using resistance training, their workouts fit into the following parameters: they typically worked out 3 to 4 times per week with each workout session lasting about 45 minutes. On average, 2 to 3 muscle groups would be exercised per workout session. Each workout consisted of between 6 to 10 exercises with each exercise being completed for 2 to 4 sets of 8 to 12 reps. Rest periods would consist of up to 2 minutes rest between each set of an exercise.

As I mentioned earlier, it is important to choose the workout style that fits your own individual goals and needs. This is the main reason why I cannot prescribe a workout for everyone who follows the *Eat Stop Eat* lifestyle.

As an example, it takes a high amount of weight, volume, and stress for a 250-pound bodybuilder to maintain a high level of muscle mass. If a 250-pound bodybuilder were to follow *Eat Stop Eat*, the amount and type of exercise that he would need to do to maintain his muscle mass would be much greater than what a 145-pound woman who hasn't previously exercised would need to do. Further, a 145-pound woman who hasn't previously exercised in this manner would see very little benefit from immediately following the bodybuilder's workout routine.

Selecting the appropriate exercise program depends on the following factors:

- Your current training status (how much you currently work out)
- Your goals (maintain or gain muscle)
- The amount of muscle mass you are currently carrying

An easy rule of thumb would be to look at the amount of exercise you were doing before you started following *Eat Stop Eat*, and make sure to slowly progress from there. Just like your nutrition program, your workout routine should revolve around the simplest and easiest methods that get you the results you want.

The Importance of Sticking with It

If you are fairly inactive, then starting a workout program may actually be very difficult. Research has suggested that as many as 50% of people who start a new exercise program will drop out within six months.[287] Most of the time people say the reason that they stop exercising is that they are tired or because of lack of time. It is very important that you stick with your program, short of becoming obsessive about exercise.

Not only will sticking to your workout program help you preserve muscle mass while you are losing body fat, but it will also keep your mood elevated. In some very interesting research published in 2008, it was found that when a group of women who exercised regularly were forced to stop exercising for 72 hours, there was a noticeable decrease in their body satisfaction and mood. The results of this study also showed that after 72 hours of non-exercise, feelings of tension, anxiety, and sluggishness were increased.[288] Of course, this is ironic considering that these are the exact reasons why most people stop working out in the first place.

This leads to the idea of a downward spiral when you quit an exercise routine. You quit because you are tired or stressed, only to become even more tired and even more

stressed, and then the spiral picks up momentum, and you end up glued to your couch unable to even think about the stress of restarting another exercise program.

When it comes to exercise, balance seems to be the key. Too much exercise and you increase the risk of overuse injuries and you could become obsessive, defining yourself as a person by your exercise program. Too little exercise and you lose the muscle maintaining and myriad of health benefits. Not only this, but you also run the risk of becoming dissatisfied with your body, as well as experience a decreased mood.

For *Eat Stop Eat* the goal is to use exercise as a tool. Doing the amount needed to preserve or build some muscle, but not becoming obsessive to the point where exercise interferes with your life. You should look forward to your next workout session, not dread it. And never let it define who you are as a person.

For this reason, I recommend keeping your exercise plans as uncomplicated as possible. Stimulate your muscle following the suggestion in the above paragraphs, allow them to recover, then repeat when you are ready.

A Note on "Cardio" Training for Weight Loss

The goal of the *Eat Stop Eat* lifestyle is to let the combination of a sensible diet and brief periods of fasting lead to a decrease in body fat, while using resistance training to maintain or increase the size of your lean body mass. While traditional cardio training will not sabotage your fat loss results from following *Eat Stop Eat*, you may be surprised to see that it doesn't typically produce as large of a fat burning benefit as you might have been led to believe. This doesn't mean that cardio is bad for you or a waste of time. Cardio training may indeed benefit your overall health, it just might not pack as much of a fat burning punch as some people wish it would.

Currently the recommendation for adults is to engage in at least 150 minutes of moderate-intensity physical activity per week.[289] This seems like a reasonable suggestion. However, I have found from both personal experience and from reviewing clinical research that the work-to-reward benefit of cardio for the purpose of burning more fat is relatively low. THIS DOES NOT MEAN THAT CARDIO DOESN'T WORK. Rather, it means you have to do a disproportionately large amount of work in the gym to receive noticeable fat-burning results. In other words, it may help with fat burning, but you better be prepared to spend a large amount time to get this benefit.

Believe it or not, most research trials examining the weight loss caused by very low-calorie diets found that adding exercise did little to increase weight loss beyond what the diet alone could achieve. In other words, when it came to the actual weight loss benefits—the diets seemed to do all the work.

Take, for instance, the research conducted by Donnelly et al. that was published in 1991. Sixty-nine obese women were put on an extreme 520-calorie-per-day diet (this is much lower than I would EVER recommend). The women were then divided into 4 groups:

- Group 1 did not exercise.
- Group 2 did endurance exercise for 60 minutes 4 days per week.
- Group 3 did strength training 4 days per week.
- Group 4 did strength training AND endurance exercises 4 days per week.

At the end of the 90-day research trial all four groups lost a large amount of bodyweight, averaging over 40 pounds of weight loss! The interesting finding was that there were no differences between the four groups in terms of the amount of weight or body fat that was lost. This is despite the massive amounts of exercising that the women in Group 4 were doing compared to Group 1!

This conclusion has been found over and over again in published research. Donnelly and co-workers did a second trial that was published in 1993 demonstrating that weight training could increase muscle size while women followed an 800-calorie-per-day diet, but it could not improve weight loss or fat loss. Similar results have been found by research conducted by Kraemer in 1997, Bryner in 1999, Janssen in 2002, and Wang in 2008, just to name a few examples. As you can see, exercising for weight loss has been studied quite extensively and repeatedly proven to be less effective than we have been led to believe.

Uncovering the reason why exercising for weight loss performs so poorly in clinical trials has proven to be very difficult. We know that extra exercise does create a larger calorie deficit (since exercise burns calories). However, this extra deficit does not seem to show up on the weight loss side of the ledger, therefore either the deficit isn't as large as we thought, or there is compensation occurring somewhere else in our lives.

We also know that people who regularly perform cardio or endurance style training become able to burn a higher amount of fat as a fuel by up regulating enzymes responsible for moving fat into their muscles, and enzymes responsible for burning that fast once it enters the muscle. In a series of human experiments, it was found over and over that while non-trained muscle only slightly increase their ability to uptake fatty acids to be used as a fuel during exercise, an endurance trained muscle can continually increase their uptake of fatty acids to a much higher degree.[290, 291] This adaptation seems to happen very quickly, becoming significant after only 8 weeks of endurance training.[292] Yet, we still do not see the extra fat loss we would expect from adding cardio to a weight loss program.

The most obvious answer is that exercise simply causes people to eat more later in the day. The saying "work up a good appetite" seems to support this idea. However, clinical research suggests that this is not the case.

A review published in 2003 suggests that men and women can tolerate exercise-induced acute energy deficits and do not compensate by eating more later in the day.[293] Other studies have found that this holds true for both lean[294] and obese[295] people.

In fact, another line of research even suggests that exercise may even help control urges to binge and eat in response to negative emotions,[296] and overall seem to have a better control of their appetite.[297]

So while it may be true for some people, research suggests that for many people, exercise does not cause you to eat more calories.

The other suggestion is that exercise can create a decreased amount of movement in the period after the exercise. In research, we call this "spontaneous physical activity."

To give you a very crude idea of the theory it would look something like this: on the days that you exercised you also spent slightly more time sitting on the couch, maybe climbed the stairs of your house a couple times less, and then took fewer overall steps. These little decreases in spontaneous physical activity may diminish some of the benefit of the exercise. This has also proven to be very difficult to measure in a research setting.

The true answer is probably a combination of all of these theories. The calorie burn from exercise is simply less than we expect (or want to believe) and small changes in both post-exercise spontaneous physical activity and even smaller increases in calorie intake all come into play in making exercise less effective than we would like.

Regardless of the illusive cause, the fact remains that exercise seems to be less effective than we would like to think. However, as I stated before, this doesn't mean exercise is useless for weight loss.

A single bout of exercise stimulates adipose tissue blood flow and fat mobilization, resulting in delivery of fatty acids to skeletal muscles at a rate well-matched to metabolic requirements. With chronic exercise (training), there are changes in adipose tissue physiology, particularly an enhanced fat mobilization during acute exercise. Epidemiological observations support the idea that physically active people have relatively low fat mass.[298]

Exercise also seems to be able to cause preferential weight loss in the visceral fat deposits, more so than either resistance exercise or simply calorie restriction.[299, 300] So for people who store a large amount of fat viscerally, exercise may be a valuable addition to their weight loss program. Perhaps exercise is not causing MORE fat loss, but rather a slightly more desirable distribution of fat loss.

The pitfall to cardio training is that just like dieting, fasting, and weight training, it is a form of stress being placed on the body, and too much stress can have deleterious effects. Indeed, chronic strenuous exercise has been connected to hypercortisolism, hypogonadism, and nutritional depletion.[301] So while the right amount of cardio can cause marked increases in insulin sensitivity and the increased ability to clear fat from your bloodstream to be used as a fuel, too much exercise can cause negative health issues, especially when coupled with a large calorie deficit.[302]

The truth is that if you get your diet in order and are following a nutrition program that allows you to decrease your caloric intake, it will cause you to lose weight. Adding calorie burning exercises does not seem to increase this weight loss to as large a degree as we would like, but may create small improvements in both weight loss and health. Adding strength training is still the number one priority for anyone attempting to lose body fat since it can preserve or even help increase the size of your muscles while you are dieting, and prevent undesirable changes in your metabolism.

However, for those people who have the time or specific need, adding extra cardio can still be an added fat loss benefit... if you have the time.

The bottom line when it comes to *Eat Stop Eat* and the *Eat Stop Eat* lifestyle is the following:

> *The simple approach is the one that works best, and this approach involves eating for fat loss and working out to preserve (or even increase) the size of your muscles. Try to be as active as possible, while also allowing yourself ample recovery time. Add cardio only if needed, only if you find it enjoyable, and have the available time.*

Other Health Benefits of Exercise

It should be obvious that maintenance of lean body mass isn't the only benefit of following a well-planned exercise program. In fact, I would argue that there are other benefits that are much more important to our overall health.

Similar to fasting and simply eating less, following a resistance training program can decrease many markers of chronic inflammation, such as IL-6, resistin, and leptin.[303] Since chronic inflammation is a risk factor in many diseases, it's no wonder why regular exercise is recommended as an anti-inflammatory therapy.[304]

The effect that exercise has on inflammatory markers does seem dependent on the intensity of exercise, training status, age, and severity of existing health conditions, but for the most part almost any form of exercise will have some form of benefit.[305]

When you combine the anti-inflammatory effects of exercise with the already mentioned benefits of improved cholesterol levels, improved blood sugar control, increased bone density, and the ability of exercise to elevate mood and self-esteem, it becomes clear that there is more to exercise then simply building muscle.[306, 307] However, the fact that proper functioning muscle may play a role in all of these factors of health cannot be denied.

Just remember exercise is a tool. Do the amount needed to preserve or build some muscle, but try your best to avoid becoming obsessive to the point where an addiction to exercise interferes with your life.

How to "Keep It Off" with Eat Stop Eat

Obviously, the goal of any weight loss program should not be quick, short-lived weight loss. To truly reap the benefits of any weight loss program the results need to be long lasting. Let's face it, nobody wants to put the effort into losing weight just so they can gain it back. Typically, maximal weight loss occurs during the first 6 months of a diet, after which, weight regain slowly begins to set in.[308]

Luckily this could be one of the greatest strengths of *Eat Stop Eat*. Let me explain.

Most research looking at long-term weight loss follows a protocol like this: get a bunch of people and make them lose weight very quickly using a very-low-calorie diet with lots of clinical supervision, rules, support groups, follow up meetings, guidelines, and checklists.

Typically, once the subjects have lost roughly 10% to 15% of their original bodyweight they go on to the weight maintenance period of the study where researchers test different ways of eating to see if some are better than others at helping people maintain or even improve upon their weight loss.

The studies have been remarkably conclusive in that the specific macronutrient profile of the diet did not matter. In other words, the amount of protein, carbohydrates, and fats in the diet does not affect how well the diet is able help you keep the weight off.

Although some randomized trials have indicated that carbohydrate-restricted diets are advantageous compared with higher-carbohydrate diets in achieving weight loss over 6 months, longer trials have shown that the advantage is not sustained beyond this time frame. Which is another way of saying that after one year, there is no significant difference in how much weight these people kept off, regardless of how high or low their carb or protein intake was.[309, 310, 311, 312]

There may be some benefit to eating slightly more protein and slightly fewer carbs in some people, but clearly it takes more than simple changes in the macronutrient composition to maintain weight loss, and a change in lifestyle must occur at the same time as a strong commitment to eating less.

In fact, research has found two things:

1   Your ability to keep the weight off is directly related to your ability to maintain a flexible amount of dietary restraint.[313]

2 Your ability to keep the weight off is directly related to how well you maintained your lean body mass while you were losing weight.[314]

Now, after reading point two you may immediately be thinking of some scientific explanation that includes the so-called "metabolism boosting" effect of lean mass. There is another just as plausible explanation to why preserving your lean body mass helps people lose weight. People will be rewarded psychologically and socially from the changes they've made in their body and be more willing to maintain dietary restraint in order keep this new body shape! In other words, having less fat and a defined lean body makes you look good, and it only takes a few compliments on your new lean toned body to keep you highly motivated to keep it up.

Regardless of why maintaining your lean body mass improves your ability to keep the weight off, the point remains: if you can follow a method of eating that allows you to eat less for long periods of time while still eating the foods you enjoy, and if you can preserve your lean body mass while you lose body fat, you greatly increase your chances of keeping the weight off!

This is the major benefit of *Eat Stop Eat*. You still eat the foods you like without restricting yourself to lists of good foods and avoiding everything on a list of bad foods. You still have to eat less, but you are in charge of the foods you choose to eat.

By being flexible and not restrictive, it allows you to enact a great deal of dietary restraint without feeling deprived or bored of your food choices. And a very large body of research suggests that this flexibility is a key to long-term weight loss success.

A large amount of epidemiological[315, 316, 317, 318] and intervention studies[319, 320] clearly point to the relative advantage of flexible restraint of calorie intake over rigid control for long-term weight loss success. Combine this with the research showing that people who used fasting as a method of weight control maintained most of their weight loss over the course of an entire year,[321] and you can see why the Eat Stop Eat lifestyle can be incredibly effective at not only helping you remove the excess weight, but keeping it off for good.

Eat Stop Eat as a Form of Physical Training

When you really stop to consider what we are trying to accomplish with *Eat Stop Eat* style fasting, it really should be considered a form of *asceticism*—a form of physical training, just like weight training, running, yoga, or any other form of exercise done for the purpose of improving one's body.

Asceticism
(from the Greek: ἄσκησις, áskēsis, "exercise" or "training")

Now, the typical use of the term *asceticism* is one that describes a life of abstinence, refraining from sensual pleasures and the accumulation of material wealth. However, the older use of the adjective "ascetic" was derived from the ancient Greek term *askēsis*, which means training or exercise.[322] So the original usage did not refer to self-denial, but to the discipline and physical training required for athletic events and this physical training often included periods of fasting.

Based on these definitions, fasting could be the purest hybrid of the two definitions; since it could be considered a **form of physical training through short-term abstinence from caloric intake.**

The description of fasting as a form of physical training is actually very logical as the act of fasting holds many similarities with the other, more well-known forms of physical training. At its root fasting, just like any other form of exercise, imposes a small stress on the body that then allows the body to adapt and become stronger (a process called hormesis). And, just like weight training or running, the proper management of that stress is critical to your long-term success.

Hormesis is the term for generally favorable biological responses to acute stresses being placed on the body. That same stress has the opposite effect when applied in too large or too long of a dose.

Hormesis
(from Greek hórmēsis "rapid motion" or "eagerness")

The term "stress" describes the state of a living organism when, under the influence of internal or external stimuli or "stressors," the dynamic equilibrium of the organism (homeostasis) is threatened.[323] In much simpler terms, stress is when you are challenged, when you have to react to something that is slightly threatening.

Exercise can be considered a form of stress because it acutely challenges multiple systems of your body, such as the cardiorespiratory system and muscular systems, forcing them to adapt and create a new dynamic equilibrium.[324] Fasting does the same, challenging multiple systems of your body to adapt to a new level of performance.

Exercise and fasting are both forms of short-term stress imposed on our bodies in order to improve our health and well-being through physical training, which under the right circumstances also cause fat loss and muscle growth as well as a whole host of other benefits. And, both exercise and fasting follow rules of hormesis—the "right" amount is good for you, but too much or too often can have the opposite effects.

In order for any form of physical training to positively affect your body you must balance the right amount of stress with the appropriate amount of rest or recovery. In other words, we want the stress to be acute—for a short, defined period of time only.

In terms of how much is the right amount I must say that I'm pretty sure there is no one-size-fits-all answer as everyone is different. All we have are guidelines, but I'll get to that in a moment.

Weight training is the perfect example of this hormetic need for balance between acute stress followed by a period of recovery. The statement, "You have to tear it down a little to build it back up," is a great representation of what actually happens with weight training.

In fact, if you were to look through a microscope and see what muscle fibers look like immediately after a weight training workout you would probably tell people to never ever weight train ever again. The damage would be immense! The fibers would be broken and disorganized, as if they had been hit by a miniature grenade.

If the training was intense enough you would also see some slight metabolic disturbances, and if it was overly intense, such as training 2 times a day for a couple of days in a row, you would see some larger metabolic disturbances. Testosterone would be lowered, cortisol increased, thyroid would also be lowered as would be your leptin levels.[325] In short, it would look like exercise was the very worst thing you could possibly do to your body.

However, if you looked at those same muscle fibers after 3 or 4 days of rest you would see something completely different, the fibers would be organized with no signs of damage, and they quite possibly could be a little bit bigger and stronger than they were before. Your hormone profile would be improved beyond where they were before you started weight training. These are the positive adaptations you get from weight training—the good things that happen AFTER the recovery from the stress.

Similar events happen with running. Immediately after a run, not only would muscle fibers be destroyed, but insulin sensitivity would be impaired and cortisol would be increased.[326] But again, with enough recovery time the lasting results would be an increased ability to burn fat, an improved metabolic profile and a better ability to run both longer distances and at a faster speed.

When you look at what happens to your body it becomes evident that any form of training is a direct stress on the body, an attack on what your body would consider to be normal. How your body adapts to this stress is what eventually gives you the health benefits associated with both exercise and fasting.

This is the basis of all forms of physical training. An "attack" must occur, and it must be bad enough to force a reaction, and then time must be given so that your body is able to recover.

Without recovery, even something as beneficial as exercise can become damaging. Chronically spending extended periods of time doing strenuous exercise without adequate recovery (a condition often found in elite athletes) can lead to hypercortisolism, hypogonadism, and can actually increase the risk of coronary heart disease.[327]

And just like exercise, fasting for too long and too often without proper recovery (periods of eating normally) can also be damaging. The end result of prolonged periods of not-eating can lead to the elimination of all body fat stores, then eventually muscle loss, and finally, if you go long enough—like a several-month-long hunger strike—then death could result.

For proper physical training to occur, the attack, stress, or insult must always be matched with recovery—and the amount of recovery needed depends on many lifestyle factors of the individual person.

Just as the true benefits of exercise come from the combination of exercise plus recovery, the true benefits of fasting come from the combination of fasting plus recovery. And this is just another of the list of similarities between fasting and exercise.

In fasting, just like in exercise, good things happen during the actual act. Things such as the increase in growth hormone and the liberation and burning of your body fat as a fuel, and still more good things happen afterwards, like the increase in muscle protein synthesis, improved insulin sensitivity, and decreased systemic inflammation.

Interestingly, sometimes things we would consider to be bad also happen during the training (fasting or exercise) as a necessary step towards the good things that happen after the training. During both resistance exercise and non-resistance exercise, muscle protein synthesis is repressed, just as it is during fasting.[328, 329, 330, 331] But after exercise, especially after resistance exercise, muscle protein synthesis is again elevated, and this elevation is increased if a meal, especially a meal containing protein is consumed.[332] Just like exercise, muscle protein synthesis is elevated after a fast, since by definition the fast only ends once a meal is consumed.

Fasting is also similar to non-resistance exercise like endurance training as it is able to train a person (both men and women, young and old) to burn more fat as a fuel.[333]

To obtain the full benefits of fasting you must temper the time spent in the fasted state against the time spent "recovering" or eating. Just as you cannot weight train for 3 to 4 hours per day every day without making significant alterations in your day-to-day life to ensure proper recovery, fasting for much longer than 24-hours without adequate recovery times afterwards simply isn't advisable for the average person— especially if you are combining the stress of fasting with the stress of weight training, running, sports, work, and everyday life.

This is why *Eat Stop Eat* has been designed as a 24-hour fast once or twice a week, allowing anywhere from 2 to 6 days for recovery between fasts.

The amount of fasting/recovery that is right for you is up to you, and it will change based on the other stresses in your life. Some weeks you may only feel like fasting once, on other weeks twice. There may even be weeks where you don't feel like fasting at all, this is okay.

Another of the main philosophies behind *Eat Stop Eat* is that once your fast is over you pretend it never happened. You go back to eating as you normally would—in a responsible way that will maintain your weight. As a general rule of thumb, I do not recommend anything under 20% calorie deficit on the days you are not fasting, nor do I recommend anything over a 20% calorie surplus, as either can be considered another additional form of stress. In other words, attempting to "recover" from a fast by grossly overeating may be just as damaging as attempting to continue a highly restricted diet in between your fasts.

However, please remember that these are only guidelines. Your ability to manage your fasts is specific to you and just as you can improve your level of fitness in any specific area of training, you can also improve your ability to fast—so even if you found fasting difficult the first couple of times it will ultimately get better as you become more "trained" at going in and out of the fasted state, and better at managing the stress.

Eat Stop Eat is a method of eating that allows for one or two small periods of "stress" per week, a form of physical training through the short-term abstinence from caloric intake. In this sense *Eat Stop Eat* is more of a style of training than it is a diet. Dieting or how you choose to eat is what you do between your fasts, but your fasts are a form of training.

The main advantage of this approach over traditional dieting is that the stress is short term and allows for ample recovery time in between stresses as opposed to normal dieting, which may include weeks if not months on end of diet induced stress on the body.

Eat Stop Eat Conclusions

By now I hope it is apparent to you that occasional short periods of intermittent fasting combined with a regular resistance-training program is an easy, uncomplicated, and highly effective way to lose weight. It can also help correct some of the negative metabolic effects that come from spending so much time in the fed state, and can improve many markers of long-term health.

To get the full benefit of *Eat Stop Eat* remember to include resistance training as part of your weight loss program and overall approach to health. How much and what style is up to you, just remember to always balance the amount of exercise you do with how much time you have to recover from that exercise.

You may also perform cardio-type exercise with *Eat Stop Eat*, just remember that while there are health benefits to this type of exercise, too much can lead to a negative impact on your health.

Never be afraid to adjust the amount you work out or how often you fast in order to maintain your energy levels and overall feelings of health. Some weeks you may fast twice, others only once. Some weeks you may lift weights four times, others you may only lift only twice. The key to keeping this lifestyle sustainable is to always remember to keep it flexible and adapt to stresses and needs of your everyday life.

Finally remember that there is no need to stack *Eat Stop Eat* on top of other, more strict forms of dieting. While many diets tout day-by-day diet plans, cookbooks, and charts of acceptable and unacceptable foods, none of this is needed when you adopt the *Eat Stop Eat* lifestyle.

Eat Stop Eat will hopefully free you from the nutrition info-clutter that surrounds us every day in the media.

My opinion is that there is ZERO relationship between how many fitness marketing emails we receive each day, how many fitness books we read, how many health forums we visit, and how much weight we lose or how healthy we feel.

Stressing over what we eat, how we workout, what to do to lose weight and all the confusion and frustration that goes along with these things no longer needs to be a part of your life. You do not need any of them to lose weight. Any message that is full of nutrition and fitness rhetoric and "eat this, not that" lists and rules that "you absolutely need to follow" is nothing more than nutritional mind-clutter.

More importantly, getting rid of this stress can actually improve your weight loss and overall health. As surprising as it sounds, "stressing" over your diet can actually make losing weight more difficult. It has been suggested that excessive psychological stress combined with overeating can actually have synergistic effects that are damaging to both your weight loss goals and long-term health.[334]

What is interesting is that the stress of excessive dietary restraint, especially when not accompanied by the act of actually eating less can increase markers of stress response within the body.[335] So when I say that "stressing" about eating healthy isn't good for you, I mean it in the most literal sense!

In fact, the reproductive hormones in both men (testosterone) and women (estrogen) are both highly responsive to not only physical stress, but mental stress as well.[336, 337] So you truly can stress yourself into compromised health. Now there is still a benefit to healthy eating. I'm not giving you an excuse to eat like a child the day after Halloween. I still recommend eating a variety of fruits and vegetables combined with some sources of protein, but I emphasize that in the *Eat Stop Eat* lifestyle, you do not have to stress over what you choose to eat.

I want you to eat in a way that is sustainable, and then to take an occasional break from eating in the form of a brief fast. It might be one fast per week, or it may be two—depending on how you are feeling.

Think of fasting as a passive approach to weight loss—allowing weight loss to happen at its own speed, as opposed to obsessive amounts of dieting and exercise which aggressively push your body to lose more and more fat, at rate that is always near the upper-limit of what your body can handle.

With fasting, we lose weight through the actions of doing nothing, or more specifically through the actions of eating nothing. We LOSE WEIGHT when we are NOT EATING. And when we eat, we enjoy eating. In fact, the *Eat Stop Eat* lifestyle can be best described by slightly altering a famous Zen quote:

> *"Before you study Zen, mountains are mountains and rivers are rivers; while you are studying Zen, mountains are no longer mountains and rivers are no longer rivers; but once you have had enlightenment, mountains are once again mountains and rivers again rivers."*

With a couple of small changes, we can sum up the *Eat Stop Eat* view of food and nutrition with one (rather long) sentence.

> *"Before you study nutrition, food is food and drink is drink; while you are studying nutrition, food is no longer food and drink is no longer drink; but once you have had enlightenment, food is once again food and drink is again drink."*

My goal is that by the end of this book, food has once again become food and drink has once again become drink for you. Hopefully you are able to enjoy the foods you eat while realizing that research has shown us conclusively that food does not have magical weight loss properties and that any food can be part of a balanced weight loss plan.

By following the *Eat Stop Eat* lifestyle you are able to lose weight by using an uncomplicated and stress-free style of eating that balances your fed and fasted metabolism. This allows you to reap the health and metabolic benefits of short periods of fasting, including weight loss, decreased inflammation, and improved metabolic profile, all while reducing the amount of time you stress about what you are eating.

The bottom line is that with *Eat Stop Eat*, we can lose weight while creating a healthier relationship with food and accepting that food is:

1   A fuel for your body when you need it.

And...

2   To be enjoyed.

From this point forward, you can enjoy the foods you eat, and enjoy knowing that with the *Eat Stop Eat* lifestyle you can lose fat, build muscle, eat every day, never follow some crazy fad diet ever again, and be 100% positive that not only is taking the occasional break from eating not bad for you, but that it actually has tremendous health benefits.

Eat less, stress less; move more, lift more, and get a good night's sleep. For physical health, that's pretty much as good as it gets.

Eat Stop Eat FAQs

Q I want to lose fat and gain some muscle. I've been told that I need to eat large amounts of protein every day to put on muscle mass. Won't fasting cause me to lose muscle?

No, as long as you are working out with strength training exercises you will not lose muscle. In fact, it is possible to gain muscle during *Eat Stop Eat*.

Q I've been trying the Eat Stop Eat lifestyle for several weeks now, but occasionally I get headaches when I'm fasting, what gives?

There has been a lot of research on Ramadan fasting and headaches. It seems that women are particularly susceptible to headaches while fasting. This is not due to dehydration,[338, 339] and may actually be similar to withdrawal symptoms, similar to the headaches you experience when you quit drinking coffee cold-turkey. From my experience, if you experience headaches they do tend to go away after your first couple of fasts. If needed, you can treat your headache as you normally would when not fasting.

Q **I'm really enjoying adding fasting into my eating plan, but I'd still like to clean up the way I eat when I'm not fasting, any tips?**

You can incorporate any diet style you like while you are following *Eat Stop Eat*. My personal opinion is that the general guideline of eating "lean and green" (along with plenty of herbs and spices) is an ideal complement to the *Eat Stop Eat* lifestyle, but you can incorporate any diet style you wish.

Q **What are things I can do other than fasting to help me lose fat?**

My recommendation would be to look for small changes you can make in the way you eat when you are not fasting. Once you have gone without food for 24 hours a few times, you really start to get a feel for the real reasons behind why you eat, what you eat, and when you eat.

Often times, hunger isn't one of these reasons. Habit and emotional connection are usually the culprits. If you take this new-found wisdom, you can create a big difference in the way you eat by making SMALL, almost unnoticeable changes in your eating habits.

Q If I start the Eat Stop Eat Lifestyle, how quickly will I lose weight?

It is a dietary truism that you can't take off in a day what you put on over years. With the *Eat Stop Eat* lifestyle, you should be able to lose weight at a rate of 1 to 2 pounds per week. However, for people who are exceptionally lean (under 9% for men and under 19% for women) weight loss tends to be slower, generally between 0.5 to 1 pound per week.

Q Do I need to take a multi-vitamin on the days that I am fasting?

No, a multi-vitamin is generally not necessary if you are eating a balanced diet. However, if you like taking multi-vitamins then by all means, continue to do so; they will not negatively affect the health benefits of fasting. Sometimes, they may need to be taken with food if you get nauseous. Since with *Eat Stop Eat*, you never go a day without eating, that is easily accommodated.

Q Will fasting affect my menstrual cycle?

Generally the answer is no, even longer fasts have been shown to have little impact on the menstrual cycle of normal weight women.[340, 341] There is research, however, to suggest that longer fasts (72 hours) can affect the menstrual cycle of exceptionally lean women (body fat levels well below 20%).[342] For this reason I do not recommend fasting for longer than 24 hours, and as always, if you do discover menstrual irregularities while losing weight please see your medical doctor or health care practitioner.

Q I read that any weight loss from fasting is only water and muscle—not fat—and you regain the weight when you start eating again. Is this true?

This is not true. During the actual period of time when you are fasting, your weight will be lower than normal. This is due to the fact that you have no food in your system, and your body has shed some excess water. However, with several periods of fasting, the weight loss you see is very real and it is indeed fat loss.

Q I've heard that under-eating will slow my metabolism down and put me in "starvation mode" which will cause me to store more fat. Will this happen with the Eat Stop Eat lifestyle?

No. On the *Eat Stop Eat* lifestyle you never go a day without food, and you spend most of your days eating your regular diet without changing anything. Your daily calories will only be lower on the days you start and finish your fast. The overall effect should come out to about a 15-25% calorie reduction over the entire week with no negative effects on your metabolism.

Q Are there any specific supplements I should take while I am fasting?

If you have been asked by a qualified health care professional to take a certain supplement, then continue to do so. However, I do not believe there is any need for extra or special supplements during your fast.

Q I've heard that short periods of fasting similar to the Eat Stop Eat lifestyle are being studied in animals. I've read it can increase their life expectancy. Is this true?

Some of the Similarities Between Fasting and Exercise

	FASTING*	EXERCISE**
Insulin	DOWN	DOWN
Growth Hormone	UP	UP
Free Fatty Acids	UP	UP
Fat Burning Potential	UP	UP
Amino Acid Movement	UP	UP
Epinephrine / Norepinephrine	UP	UP
Cortisol	UP	UP
Leptin	DOWN	DOWN
Autophagy	UP	UP

Data from short-term fasting 12-36 hours in men and women.

** *Data from both resistance exercise and non-resistance exercise.*

Yes. As a matter of fact, this research is being done by Dr. Mark Mattson at the National Institute on Aging. Research suggests that animal's age slower and live longer when they consume fewer calories. The research is showing that this effect can be achieved by eating less each day, or by fasting on intermittent days.[343]

Q Why do I have to fast for 24 hours? Couldn't I just do 18 hours, or 36 if I wanted more results?

The answer is twofold. First: according to the research, the 24-hour point is right in the middle of the maximum adaptation for fat burning. Second: through trial and error, many of my initial test subjects (including me) following an *Eat Stop Eat* lifestyle found that 24 hours was the least intrusive to their daily lifestyle. A 24-hour period made the most sense from a practical and scientific stand point.

In actuality, your body begins to burn significantly more fat four to eight hours after your last meal (depending on the size of your last meal). This effect begins to level off after 30 hours. If you don't quite make it to the 24-hour point some days, don't sweat it. You're still getting a benefit.

I do not recommend extended fasts by a considerable amount past the 24-hour mark because I believe they become too intrusive on a person's lifestyle. There is nothing wrong with cutting a fast short at 22 hours, or extending a fast to 25 or 26 hours if it fits into your schedule. However, if you end up fasting for 40, 50, or even 70 hours I simply do not see how this CANNOT become intrusive n your life. By extending your fasts into the range of 2 to 3 days, you lose the flexibility that makes *Eat Stop Eat* so effective as a long-term weight loss solution. So as a rule of thumb, if I had to pick between fasting for shorter or longer periods of time, I'd rather you fast for less time, than to fast for more time.

Q **I I heard breakfast is the most important meal of the day. Will it affect me if I miss breakfast on a fast day?**

There is no scientific evidence to prove that breakfast is any more important than lunch or dinner for adults. As a matter of fact, there is no scientific evidence proving three meals per day are any better than eating five, or one meal per day.

Q **Can I follow the Eat Stop Eat Lifestyle if I am pregnant?**

No. *Eat Stop Eat* should not be used by anyone who is pregnant or trying to get pregnant. After your pregnancy, consult your physician to see if *Eat Stop Eat* is suitable for you and your individual circumstances.

Q **I know that black coffee, diet soda pop, and water are fine during my fasting periods, but what about sugar-free gum?**

I have used sugar-free gum during my fasts. Most of these gums contain 2 to 3 calories per piece, so I consider a couple of pieces of gum to be acceptable during a fast.

Q **I'm a bodybuilder and I'm interested in trying fasting. Can I still take any of my supplements on the fasting day (I'm trying to gain muscle)?**

Lucky for you, the one supplement that is proven to increase strength and muscle mass in the long term is creatine mono-hydrate. And, since creatine is not metabolized for energy and does not raise insulin levels, taking creatine on your fasting days is perfectly acceptable (but I would still recommend taking your creatine at the times when you are eating).

Q I know you suggest weight training while following the Eat Stop Eat lifestyle, but what about other types of exercise like yoga or mountain biking?

I absolutely encourage you to practice as many different types of exercise as possible. Just like nutrition, I think variety is the key to exercise and both yoga and mountain biking are excellent examples of exercises that complement the *Eat Stop Eat* lifestyle. As long as you are doing some form of resistance training at least two or three times a week, you can add any additional exercises you wish.

Q My daughter is 14 and overweight, can she try the Eat Stop Eat lifestyle?

Unfortunately, no, she cannot. All of the research conducted on fasting is done on adults; there is no way for me to know its effects on children. I only recommend *Eat Stop Eat* for healthy adults.

Q Do you think the Eat Stop Eat lifestyle would be beneficial to someone who is simply trying to maintain his or her current weight?

Yes. *Eat Stop Eat* provides a simple way to maintain your weight. Instead of fasting once every 3 to 5 days, a person wishing to maintain their bodyweight could fast once every 6 to 8 days.

Q **I've read that you need to eat every two to three hours in order to prevent your blood sugar from crashing, how does Eat Stop Eat affect my blood sugar?**

The truth about having low blood sugar is that it is not nearly as common as we are often led to believe. People who suffer from true hypoglycemia typically have a "hypoglycemia disorder." This disorder is usually diagnosed by a medical test. What's more, true hypoglycemia isn't just feeling tired but includes confusion, difficulty speaking, and even seizures and convulsions.[344] For the vast majority of the healthy population, we are easily able to maintain healthy blood sugars that are neither too high nor too low in a whole range of different situations, including fasting and intense exercise.

In research examining the effects of a 24-hour fast, it was found that fasting did not cause blood sugar levels to dip below 3.5 mmol/Liter, meaning that during the entire 24-hour fast, blood sugar slowly lowered itself, but remained at normal non-hypoglycemic levels.[345]

Q **My Dad is really interested in Eat Stop Eat, but he is diabetic. Can he still try the Eat Stop Eat lifestyle?**

Eat Stop Eat was designed for healthy people trying to lose weight. If your father wants to try *Eat Stop Eat*, he should only do so under the direct supervision of a doctor or healthcare practitioner.

Q In the beginning of Eat Stop Eat you say that it can improve your health and "might just save your life," these are some pretty bold statements. What gives?

Right now, there is ongoing research on short-term fasting and its ability to improve certain markers of health. While it would be premature of me to say that fasting can help with a medical condition, I can say that it has been used with success in clinical research on people who suffer from asthma,[346] lowers inflammation,[347] and is being studied for its potential to improve brain health.[348]

Q What about post-workout nutrition? Don't I need to eat immediately after my workouts?

According to Dr. Michael Rennie of the University of Nottingham, the idea that there is golden period of getting amino acids into your muscles is speculative at best. What's more, the American College of Sports Medicine recommends that athletes who take a day or two to rest between vigorous workout sessions do not need to worry about the timing of carbohydrate intake. The bottom line is that most of today's post-workout nutrition advice serves three purposes—to possibly (please note the vagueness of that term) support the muscle building process in young (university-aged) men and women who are just starting a workout program, to fuel the metabolic needs of ELITE athletes, and to help sell sports supplements. You can work out on your fasting days without having to worry about your post-workout nutrition.

Q With all the news about sugar being bad for you, shouldn't I be cutting down on the amount of sugar I eat if I want to lose weight?

You should, and you are. Think of it this way, if you are very diligent and watch the foods you eat day in and day out, skip desserts, and avoid many of the high sugar foods you normally eat, you might be able to reduce your sugar intake by 30%.

Alternatively, you could keep eating the way you normally eat, and fast for two 24-hour periods over the course of a week, and still reduce your sugar intake by 30%. By fasting for two days out of seven, you automatically reduce your sugar intake by about 30%, just by missing two 24-hour periods of eating. The *Eat Stop Eat* lifestyle is a great way to get the exact same result as a restrictive diet WITHOUT spending day after day monitoring every piece of food you put into your mouth.

Q I've read that high-protein diets can help with weight loss. Can I eat high protein while doing Eat Stop Eat?

Yes. There are several published research studies suggesting that a higher amount of dietary protein might be associated with an increased rate of weight loss (as long as the diet is calorie reduced). Most of the research I've reviewed have had people eat between 70 and 150 grams of protein per day (not the crazy 250 grams of protein per day suggestions that you find in fitness magazines). If you like, you can definitely try eating a higher protein diet while using *Eat Stop Eat*.

Q What is the best thing for me to eat after I am finished fasting?

When you finish your fast you need to pretend that your fast NEVER HAPPENED. No compensation, no reward, no special way of eating, no special shakes, drinks, or pills. The minute you decide to stop fasting, you need to wipe the fast from your memory, and eat the exact way you would normally eat at that specific time of the day (while eating responsibly of course). If you end your fast at dinnertime, have dinner. If you end your fast at 4:00 PM and you don't typically have dinner until 6:00 or 7:00 PM, then have a light snack... but nothing larger than you would normally have at that time.

There is no magic way to end your fast. The absolute best thing you can do is simply pretend your fast never happened and begin eating in the exact way you would normally eat at that specific time of day.

Q Can I have a little bit of non-fat milk in my coffee while I am fasting?

Unfortunately, my answer is no. I would recommend you try to fast without making little concessions in your diet. While I do admit that small amounts of calories probably will not interrupt the fasting state metabolism, I am still concerned that fat free (non-fat) milk still has too many calories for when you are fasting. Stick with calorie-free beverages as much as possible while you fast. My answer would be the same for a small amount of cream or sugar.

Q **Can I drink juice while I am fasting?**

I do not recommend drinking any juice while you are fasting. From my experience, using a juice fast for weight loss can be disastrous. Remember, the key to *Eat Stop Eat* is to try and consume NO calories for 24 hours.

Juice is high in calories, so it is like drinking liquid food, and much less filling... if you think about it, this is actually depressing. You get the calories without the pleasure. In my opinion, this defeats the whole purpose.

Q **I want to fast every day except weekends, does it make a difference if my fast lasts for 23 hours instead of 24 hours?**

I don't think there is a large difference between 23 and 24 hours. That being said, I must say that I do not endorse the practice of fasting for such a large length every single day. The point of *Eat Stop Eat* is to add flexibility to your diet plan, not remove flexibility, which is essentially what spending 23 hours of fasting every day would do. I urge you to try fasting once or twice a week first, I'm sure you will be surprised by the effectiveness of this simple approach.

Q **I was wondering if there was any research on the effects of fasting on a women's menstrual cycle?**

There is some research that looked at the effect of short-term fasting on the menstrual cycle of women. These research studies found that despite the metabolic changes that occur during fasting, even fasts as long as 72 hours do not seem to have an effect on the menstrual cycle of normal cycling women.[349] However, if you have any questions or concerns about your menstrual cycle you should discuss them with your doctor or health care practitioner.

Q So, are you saying that (insert newest style of eating here) is wrong?

No, not at all. There is no wrong way to eat. The only thing that can be wrong, or scientifically incorrect, is the explanation of the benefits of a particular way of eating, or the reasons why one type of eating is 'better' than another type of eating.

Q What about post-workout nutrition—do you think it is necessary to have high glycemic carbohydrates after training?

I really don't see any need for high-glycemic carbs after training unless you are an endurance athlete and need to replenish glycogen stores. Even then, it would only be if you have to compete again in very short period of time (24 to 48 hours). For general muscle growth and well-being, I think carbs are one of the most overrated post-workout foods. With typical eating, your glycogen stores will be replenished to their maximum within 48 hours after your workout.

Unless you are doing multiple endurance style events in the same day, I see emphasis on high-carbohydrate intake as just another obsessive-compulsive eating habit that can wind up causing us to gain weight.

Q I really enjoy the idea of a cheat day while I'm dieting. Can I do a cheat day with Eat Stop Eat?

I really don't see any reason why you can't. If you want to have a big day of eating every once in a while, and if this makes you happy, then I am all for it with three reservations:

1 As long as your overall calorie intake averaged over the week remains low.

2 The cheat day doesn't make you feel guilty or depressed the next day.

3 You aren't force-feeding yourself to the point of feeling sick in the hopes of having some beneficial health or fat-loss effect.

Q Sometimes when I fast my fingertips get cold, why is that?

Fasting increases the blood flow to your body fat (the process is called adipose tissue blood flow).[350] So when you are fasting more blood is travelling to your body fat, presumably to help move it to your muscles where it can be burned as a fuel. Due to this increased travel to your body fat, vaso-constriction occurs in your fingertips and sometimes toes to compensate. So, in some cases it's a "necessary evil" in the fat loss process.

Q I noticed you said that chronic inflammation can negatively affect muscle building, but I heard that taking high doses of anti-inflammatory after your workout can also negatively affect muscle building... I'm confused.

While CHRONIC inflammation can negatively affect the muscle building process, ACUTE inflammation seems to be involved in the muscle building process in a positive way. So, the difference lies in chronic being bad, while the proper type of acute inflammation may indeed be beneficial. (Also keep in mind that those studies on anti- inflammatory drugs having a negative effect on muscle building were using very high doses[351], studies on lower doses did not show this same affect.[352])

Q **What is your opinion on taking branched chain amino acids during a fast?**

The branched chain amino acids leucine, isoleucine, and valine are a family of essential amino acids that are extremely important to muscle physiology — including growth and repair. The BCAAs (specifically leucine) act through a protein-signaling pathway regulated by something called mTor to initiate the process of protein synthesis, which at times can initiate the process of muscle growth. While some people recommend BCAAs during a fast to prevent muscle loss, I see some issues with this suggestion.

To start, there is little evidence to suggest muscle loss should be a concern during short-term fasting. Secondly, mTOR is not exclusive to muscle, it is found in almost every cell in the body, and plays an important role in dozens of processes within the human body. The main reason I do not recommend BCAA intake during a fast is that mTOR is a strong negative regulator of autophagy[353] (see the chapter on cellular cleansing), and even small doses of BCAA can increase insulin (another negative regulator of autophagy) and initiate mTOR driven decreases in autophagy.[354] So there seems to be very little benefit to BCAA supplementation during a fast, considering that you may be eliminating the health benefits of the fast. Better to keep your BCAAs to the end of your fast and during the times you are eating.

Q **Sometimes when I fast my stomach growls any tips to avoid this?**

Yes, for some reason I find sparkling water (Pellegrino, Perrier) tends to help. I'm not sure why, but it tends to calm a growly stomach.

Q **You never actually say how I should eat on days I'm not fasting? Should I still eat 6 times per day?**

You should eat in the way that fits your lifestyle best, while allowing you to keep calories under control and still be able to eat the foods you enjoy. If you review the body of scientific literature on eating frequency (how many times you eat in a day) you find very unremarkable results in either direction.

Forcing people to eat more often can be disastrous as some researchers have speculated that our growing obesity crisis can be blamed on eating more often as much as it can on increased portion sizes.[355] However, forcing someone to eat less frequently may end in increased portion sizes. Based on this I cannot offer a "perfect" way to eat because it simply does not exist. You have to find what works for you right now, and be willing to change the way you eat as your life changes.

Q **I've heard that people are using fasting with chemo-therapy treatments, why is this?**

Fasting is being studied as an addition to chemotherapy as very preliminary studies have found that fasting seems to reduce the side-effects typically associated with chemother-apy, including fatigue, weakness, and gastrointestinal side effects.[356] However, much further research is needed before short-term fasting becomes a recommendation for patients undergoing chemo.

Q **I'd like to fast twice a week, but I'm worried about missing my post-workout meal, can you help me?**

Without going into the science for and against the idea of post-workout meals, I will say that if you are fasting twice per week, and training less than 5 times per week, you should be able to always find a way to time your fasts and workouts so you can always have a post-workout meal. In fact, I would go so far as to say that if you are finding it difficult to fit your post-workout nutrition around you fasts you are probably being either too inflexible with your fasting routine or too inflexible with your workout routine.

REFERENCES

1   Swinburn B, Sacks G, Ravussin E. Increased food energy supply is more than sufficient to explain the US epidemic of obesity. *Am J Clin Nutr*. 2009;90:1453-6.

2   Li C, Ford ES, Zhao G, Balluz LS, Giles WH. Estimates of body composition with dual-energy X-ray absorptiometry in adults. *Am J Clin Nutr*. 2009;90(6):1457-65.

3   Adams KM, Kohlmeier M, Zeisel SH. Nutrition Education in U.S. Medical Schools: Latest Update of a National Survey. *Academic Medicine*. 2010;85(9):1537-1542.

4   Nestle, Marion. Eating Made Simple. *Scientific American Magazine*. September 2007.

5   Nestle, Marion. *What to Eat*. New York: North Point Press 2006. (For more information visit *www.whattoeatbook.com*)

6   University of Guelph, Unpublished Research, in Review.

7   Nestle, Marion. *Food politics*. Los Angeles, California: University of California Press. 2003.

8   Wansink, Brian. *Marketing Food*. Champaign, Illinois: University of Illinois Press. 2005.

9   Campos, Paul. *The Obesity Myth*. New York: Gotham Books. 2004.

10 Cunneen SA. Review of meta-analytic comparisons of bariatric surgery with a focus on laparoscopic adjustable gastric banding. *Surgery for Obesity and Related Diseases*. 2008;4:S47-S55.

11 Buchwald H, Avidor Y, Braunwald E, et al. Bariatric surgery a systematic review and meta-analysis. *Journal of the American Medical Association*. 2004;292:1724-37.

12 Webber J, Macdonald IA. The cardiovascular, metabolic and hormonal changes accompanying acute starvation in men and women. *British Journal of Nutrition*. 1994;71:437-447.

13 Heilbronn LK, et al. Alternate-day fasting in non-obese subjects: Effects on body weight, body composition, and energy metabolism. *American Journal of Clinical Nutrition.* 2005;81:69-73.

14 Bryner RW. Effects of resistance training vs. Aerobic training combined with an 800 calorie liquid diet on lean body mass and resting metabolic rate. *Journal of the American College of Nutrition* 1999;18(1):115-121.

15 Keim NL, Horn WF. Restrained eating behavior and the metabolic response to dietary energy restriction in women. *Obesity Research.* 2004;12:141-149.

16 Verboeket-Van De Venne WPHG, et al. Effect of the pattern of food intake on human energy metabolism. *British Journal of Nutrition.* 1993;70:103-115.

17 Bellisle F, et al. Meal Frequency and energy balance. *British Journal of Nutrition.* 1997;77: (Suppl. 1) s57-s70.

18 Gjedsted J, et al. Effects of a 3-day fast on regional lipid and glucose metabolism in human skeletal muscle and adipose tissue. *Acta Physiologica Scandinavia* 2007;191:205-216.

19 Gardner CD, et al. Comparison of the Atkins, Zone, Ornish, and LEARN diets on change in weight and related risk factors among overweight premenopausal women. The A to Z weight loss study: A randomized trial. *Journal of the American Medical Association.* 2007;297(9):969-998.

20 Hultman E. Physiological role of muscle glycogen in man, with special reference to exercise. *Circ Res* 1967;20(suppl 1):199-114.

21 Knapik JJ, Jones BH, Meredith C, Evans WJ. Influence of a 3.5 day fast on physical performance. *European Journal of Applied Physiology and Occupational Physiology* 1987;56(4):428-32.

22 Schisler JA, Ianuzzo CD. Running to maintain cardiovascular fitness is not limited by short-term fasting or enhanced by carbohydrate supplementation. *Journal of Physical Activity and Health.* 2007 Jan;4(1):101- 12.

23 Knapik JJ, Meredith CN, Jones LS, Young VR, Evans WJ. Influence of fasting on carbohydrate and fat metabolism during rest and exercise in men. *Journal of Applied Physiology* 1998;64(5):1923-1929.

24 Nieman DC, et al. Running endurance in 27-h-fasted humans. *Journal of Applied Physiology* 1987;63(6):2502-2509.

25 Zinker BA, Britz K, Brooks GA. Effects of a 36-hour fast on human endurance and substrate utilization. *Journal Applied Physiology* 1990;69(5):1849-1855.

26 Aragon-Vargas LF. Effects of fasting on endurance exercise. *Sports Med* 1993;16:255-65.

27   Gleeseon M, Greenhaff PL, Maughan RJ. Influence of a 24 h fast on a high intensity cycle exercise performance in man. *Eur J Appl Physiol Occup* Physiol 1988;46:211-19.

28   Dohm, GL, Beeker RT, Israel RG, Tapscott EB. Metabolic responses to exercise after fasting. *Journal of Applied Physiology* 1986;61(4):1363-1368.

29   Hermansen L, Vaage O. Lactate disappearance and glycogen synthesis in human muscle after maximal exercise. *Am J Physiol* 1977;233:E422-9.

30   Muthayya S, Thomas T, Srinivasan K, Rao K, Kurpad AV, van Klinken JW, Owen G, de Bruin EA. Consumption of a mid-morning snack improves memory but not attention in school children. *Physiology & Behavior.* 2007 Jan 30;90(1):142-50.

31   Green MW, Elliman NA, Rogers, PJ. Lack of effect of short-term fasting on cognitive function. *Journal of Psychiatric Research* 1995;29(3),245-253.

32   Lieberman HR, Caruso CM, Niro PJ, Adam GE, Kellogg MD, Nindl B, Kramer FM. A double-blind, placebo-controlled test of 2 d of calorie deprivation: effects on cognition, activity, sleep, and interstitial glucose concentrations. *American Journal of Clinical Nutrition* 2008;88:667-76.

33   Green MW, Rogers PJ, Elliman NA, Gatenby SJ. Impairment of cognitive performance associated with dieting and high levels of dietary restraint. *Physiology and Behavior.* 1994;55(3):447-52.

34   Green MW, Rogers PJ. Impaired cognitive functioning during spontaneous dieting. *Psychological Medicine.* 1995;25(5):1003-10.

35   Witte AV, Fobker M, Gellner R, Knecht S, Flöel A. Caloric restriction improves memory in elderly humans. *The Proceedings of the National Academy of Sciences.* 2009 Jan 27;106(4):1255-60.

36   Bryner RW. Effects of resistance training vs. Aerobic training combined with an 800 calorie liquid diet on lean body mass and resting metabolic rate. *Journal of the American College of Nutrition* 1999;18(1):115-121.

37   Rice B, Janssen I, Hudson, R, Ross R. Effects of aerobic or resistance exercise and/or diet on glucose tolerance and plasma insulin levels in obese men. *Diabetes Care* 1999;22:684-691.

38   Janssen I, et al. Effects of an energy-restrictive diet with or without exercise on abdominal fat, intermuscular fat, and metabolic risk factors in obese women. *Diabetes Care* 2002;25:431-438.

39   Chomentowski P, et al. Moderate exercise attenuates the loss of skeletal muscle mass that occurs with intentional caloric restriction – induced weight loss in older, overweight to obese adults. *Journal of Gerontology: Medical Sciences.* 2009;64(5):575-580.

40 Marks BL, Ward A, Morris DH, Castellani J, and Rippe RM. Fat-free mass is maintained in women following a moderate diet and exercise program. *Medicine and Science in Sports and Exercise*. 1995;27(9):1243-51.

41 Gjedsted J, Gormsen L, Buhl M, Norrelund H, Schmitz, Keiding S, Tonnesen E, Moller N. Forearm and leg amino acids metabolism in the basal state and during combined insulin and amino acid stimulation after a 3-day fast. *Acta Physiologica*. 2009;6:1-9.

42 Neel JV. Diabetes Mellitus: A "thrifty" genotype rendered detrimental by progress? *The American Journal of Human Genetics*. 1962;14:353-362.

43 Gibala MJ, Interisano SA, Tarnopolsky MA et al. Myofibrillar disruption following acute concentric and eccentric resistance exercise in strength-trained men. *Can J Physiol Pharmacol* 2000;78:656–661.

44 Bray GA, Smith SR, De Jonge L, Xie H, Rood J, Martin CK, Most M, Brock C, Mancuso S, Redman LM. Effect of dietary protein content on weight gain, energy expenditure, and body composition during overeating. *JAMA*. 2012;307(1):47-55.

45 Deldicque L, De Bock K, Maris M, Ramaekers M, Nielens H, Francaux M, Hespel P. Increased p70s6k phosphorylation during intake of a protein-carbohydrate drink following resistance exercise in the fasted state. *Eur J Appl Physiol*. 2010 Mar;108(4):791-800.

46 Samer W. El-Kadi, Agus Suryawan, Maria C. Gazzaneo, Neeraj Srivastava, Renán A. Orellana, Hanh V. Nguyen, Gerald E. Lobley, and Teresa A. Davis. Anabolic signaling and protein deposition are enhanced by intermittent compared with continuous feeding in skeletal muscle of neonates. *Am J Physiol Endocrinol Metab* 2012;302 E674-E686.

47 Van Proeyen K, De Bock K, Hespel P. Training in the fasted state facilitates re-activation of eEF2 activity during recovery from endurance exercise. *Eur J Appl Physiol*. 2011 Jul;111(7):1297-305.

48 Phillips SM, Tipton KD, Aarsland A et al. Mixed muscle protein synthesis and breakdown after resistance exercise in humans. *Am J Physiol* 1997;273(1 Pt 1),E99–107.

49 Samer W. El-Kadi, Agus Suryawan, Maria C. Gazzaneo, Neeraj Srivastava, Renán A. Orellana, Hanh V. Nguyen, Gerald E. Lobley, and Teresa A. Davis. Anabolic signaling and protein deposition are enhanced by intermittent compared with continuous feeding in skeletal muscle of neonates. *Am J Physiol Endocrinol Metab* 2012;302 E674-E686.

50 Rasmussen BB, Tipton KD, Miller SL, Wolf SE, Wolfe RR. An oral essential amino acid-carbohydrate supplement enhances muscle protein anabolism after resistance exercise. *J Appl Physiol*. 2000;88;386-392.

51 Tipton KD, Rasmussen BB, Miller SL, Wolf SE, Owens-Stovall SK, Petrini BE, Wolfe RR. Timing of amino acid-carbohydrate ingestion alters anabolic response of muscle to resistance exercise. *Am J Physiol Endocrinol Metab*. 2001 Aug;281(2):E197-206.

52 Burd NA, West DW, Moore DR, Atherton PJ, Staples AW, Prior T, Tang JE, Rennie MJ, Baker SK, Phillips SM. Enhanced amino acid sensitivity of myofibrillar protein synthesis persists for up to 24h after resistance exercise in young men. *J Nutr*. 2011 Apr 1;141(4):568-73.

53 Phillips SM, Tipton KD, Aarsland A, Wolf SE, Wolfe RR. Mixed muscle protein synthesis and breakdown after resistance exercise in humans. *Am J Physiol* 1997;273(36):E99-E107.

54 Wansink, Brian. *Mindless Eating*. New York: Bantam Dell (A division of Random House, Inc.) 2006.

55 Agatston, Arthur. *The South Beach Diet*. New York, New York: Rodale Inc. 2003.

56 Grimm O. Addicted to food. *Scientific American Mind* 2007;18(2):36-39.

57 Ozelli KL (Interviewing Volkow ND). This is your brain on food. *Scientific American Magazine*. September, 2007.

58 Rogers PJ, Smith HJ. Food cravings and food "addiction": A critical review of the evidence from a biopsychosocial perspective. *Pharmacology biochemistry and Behavior* 2000;66(1):3-14.

59 Lowe MR, Butryn ML. Hedonic hunger: A new dimension of appetite? *Physiol Behav* 2007;91:432–439.

60 Honma KL, Honma S, Hiroshige T. Critical role of food amount for prefeeding cortcosterone peak in rats. *American Journal of Physiology*. 1983;245:R339-R344.

61 Comperatore CA, Stephan FK. Entrainment of duodenal activity to periodic feeding. *Journal of Biological Rhythms*. 1987;2:227-242.

62 Stephan FK. The "other" circadian system: Food as a Zeitgeber *Journal of Biological Rhythms*. 2002; 17:284-292.

63 Steffens AB. Influence of the oral cavity on insulin release in the rat. *AM J Physiol* 1976;230:1411-1415.

64 Johnstone AM, Faber P, Gibney ER, Elia M, Horgan G, Golden BE, Stubbs RJ. Effect of an acute fast on energy compensation and feeding behavior in lean men and women. *Int J Obes Relat Metab Disord*. 2002 Dec;26(12):1623-8.

65 Guettier JM, Gorden P. Hypoglycemia. *Endocrinology Clinics of North America*. 2006;35:753–766.

66 Wiesli P, Schwegler B, Schmid B, Spinas GA, Schmid C. Mini-mental state examination is superior to plasma glucose concentrations in monitoring patients with suspected hypoglycemic disorders

during the 72-hour fast. *European Journal of Endocrinology* 2005;152:605–610.

67 Alken J, et al. Effect of fasting on young adults who have symptoms of hypoglycemia in the absence of frequent meals. *European Journal of Clinical Nutrition* 2008;62:721–726.

68 Halaas J, Gajiwala K, Maffei M, Cohen S, Chait B, et al. Weight-reducing effects of the plasma protein encoded by the obese gene. *Science* 1995;269:543–46.

69 Chan JL, et al. Short-term fasting-induced autonomic activation and changes in catecholamine levels are not mediated by changes in leptin levels in healthy humans. Clinical Endocrinology 2007;66:49–57.

70 Rosenbaum M, et al. Effects of weight change on plasma leptin concentrations and energy expenditure. *Journal of Clinical Endocrinology and Metabolism* 1997;82:3647–3654.

71 Rosenbaum M et al. Low dose leptin administration reverses effects of sustained weight reduction on energy expenditure and circulating concentrations of thyroid hormones. *The Journal of Clinical Endocrinology & Metabolism* 2002;87(5):2391–2394.

72 Ahima RS, Flier JS. Leptin. *Annual Review of Physiology*. 2000;62:413-37.

73 Kolaczynski JW, Considine RV, Ohannesian J, Marco C, Opentanova I, Nyce MR, Myint M, Caro JF. Responses of leptin to short-term fasting and refeeding in humans: a link with ketogenesis but not ketones themselves. *Diabetes*. 1996;45(11):1511-5.

74 Brennan AM, Mantzoros CS. Drug insight: the role of leptin in human physiology and pathophysiology: emerging clinical applications in leptin deficient states. *Nature Clinical Practice Endocrinology & Metabolism*. 2006;2:318-27.

75 Hislop MS, Ratanjee BD, Soule SG, Marais AD. Effects of anabolic-androgenic steroid use or gonadal testosterone suppression on serum leptin concentration in men. *European Journal of Endocrinology* 1999:141;40–46.

76 Harle P, Straub RH. Leptin is a link between adipose tissue and inflammation. *Annals of the New York Academy of Sciences* 2006;1069:454-462.

77 Horio N et al. New frontiers in gut nutrient sensor research: nutrient sensors in the gastrointestinal tract: modulation of sweet taste sensitivity by leptin. *J Pharmacol Sci*. 2010;112(1):8-12.

78 Baker HWG, Santen RJ, Burger HG, De Krester DM, Hudson B, Pepperell RJ, Bardin CW. Rhythms in the secretion of gonadotropins and gonadal steroids. *Journal of Steroids Biochemistry*, 1975;6:793-801.

79 Habito RC, Ball M. Postprandial changes in sex hormones after meals of different composition. *Metabolism* 2001;50:505–511.

80 Habito RC, Montalto J, Leslie E, Ball MJ. Effects of replacing meat with soybean in the diet on sex hormone concentrations in healthy adult males. *Br J Nutr* 2000;84:557–563.

81 Meikle AW, Stringham JD, Woodward MG, Mcmurry MP. Effects of a fat-containing meal on sex hormones in men. *Metabolism* 1990;39:943–946.

82 Volek JS, Gomez AL, Love DM, Avery NG, Sharman MJ, Kraemer WJ. Effects of a high-fat diet on postabsorptive and postprandial testosterone responses to a fat-rich meal. *Metabolism* 2001;50:1351–1355.

83 Garrel DR, Todd KS, Pugeat MM, Calloway DH. Hormonal changes in normal men under marginally negative energy balance. *Am J Clin Nutr* 1984;39:930-936.

84 Mohr BA, Bhasin S. Link CL, O'Donnell AB and McKinlay JB. The effect of changes in adiposity on testosterone levels in older men: longitudinal results from the Massachusetts Male Aging Study. *European Journal of Endocrinology*. 2006;155:443-452.

85 Derby CA, Zilber S, Brambilla D, Morales KH, McKinlay JB. Body mass index, waist circumference and waist to hip ratio and change in sex steroid hormones: the Massachusetts Male Ageing Study. *Clin Endocrinol* (Oxf). 2006 Jul;65(1):125-31.

86 Strain GW, Zumoff B, Miller LK, Rosner W, Levit C, Kalin M, Hershcopf RJ, Rosenfeld RS. Effect of massive weight loss on hypothalamic-pituitary-gonadal function in obese men. *J Clin Endocrinol Metab*. 1988 May;66(5):1019-23.

87 Pritchard J, Després JP, Gagnon J, Tchernof A, Nadeau A, Tremblay A, Bouchard C. Plasma adrenal, gonadal, and conjugated steroids following long-term exercise-induced negative energy balance in identical twins. *Metabolism*. 1999 Sep;48(9):1120-7.

88 Khoo J, Piantadosi C, Worthley S, Wittert GA. Effects of a low-energy diet on sexual function and lower urinary tract symptoms in obese men. *Int J Obes* (Lond) 2010;34:1396–403.

89 Cangemi R, Friedmann AJ, Holloszy JO, Fontana L, Long-term effects of calorie restriction on serum sex- hormone concentrations in men. *Aging Cell* 2010;9:236-242.

90 Friedl KE, Moore RJ, Hoyt RW, Marchitelli LJ, Martinez-Lopez LE, Askew EW. Endocrine markers of semistarvation in healthy lean men in a multistressor environment. *J Appl Physiol*. 2000 May;88(5):1820- 30.

91 Röjdmark S. Influence of short-term fasting on the pituitary-testicular axis in normal men. *Hormone Research*. 1987;25(3):140-6.

92 Bergendahl M, Aloi JA, Iranmanesh A, Mulligan TM, Veldhuis JD. Fasting suppresses pulsatile luteinizing hormone (LH) secretion and enhances orderliness of LH release in young but not older men. *J Clin Endocrinol Metab.* 1998 Jun;83(6):1967-75.

93 [*Merck Manual* 1992].

94 Klibanski A, Beitins IZ, Badger T, Little R, McArthur JW. Reproductive function during fasting in men. *Journal of Clinical Endocrinology and Metabolism.* 1981;53(2):258-63.

95 Chennaoui M, Desgorces F, Drogou C, Boudjemaa B, Tomaszewski A, Depiesse F, Burnat P, Chalabi H, Gomez-Merino D. Effects of Ramadan fasting on physical performance and metabolic, hormonal, and inflammatory parameters in middle-distance runners. *Applied Physiology Nutrition and Metabolism.* 2009; 34(4):587-94.

96 Röjdmark S, Asplund A, Rössner S. Pituitary-testicular axis in obese men during short-term fasting. *Acta Endocrinol* (Copenh). 1989 Nov;121(5):727-32.

97 Klibanski A, Beitins IZ, Badger T, Little R, McArthur JW. Reproductive function during fasting in men. *J Clin Endocrinol Metab.* 1981 Aug;53(2):258-63.

98 Klibanski A, Beitins IZ, Badger T, Little R, McArthur JW. Reproductive function during fasting in men.*J Clin Endocrinol Metab 1981*; 53:258.

99 Roemmich JN and Sinning WE. Weight loss and wrestling training: effects on growth-related hormones. *J Appl Physiol* 1997;82:1760–1764.

100 Friedl KE, Moore RJ, Hoyt RW, Marchitelli LJ, Martinez-Lopez LE, Askew EW. Endocrine markers of semistarvation in healthy lean men in a multistressor environment. *J Appl Physiol.* 2000; 88(5):1820–1830.

101 Hoehn K, Marieb EN. *Human Anatomy & Physiology.* San Francisco: Benjamin Cummings, 2010.

102 Munck A, Naray-Fejes-Toth A. Glucocorticoids and stress: Permissive and suppressive actions. Ann *N Y Acad Sci* 1994;746:115–130.

103 Soules MR, Merriggiola MC, Steiner RA, Clifton DK, Toivola B, Bremner WJ. Short-Term fasting in normal women: absence of effects on gonadotrophin secretion and the menstrual cycle. *Clinical Endocrinology* 1994;40:725-731.

104 Gjedsted J, Gormsen L, Buhl M, Norrelund H, Schmitz, Keiding S, Tonnesen E, Moller N. Forearm and leg amino acids metabolism in the basal state and during combined insulin and amino acid stimulation after a 3-day fast. *Acta Physiologica.* 2009;6:1-9.

105 Bergendahl M, Vance ML, Iranmanesh A, Thorner MO, Veldhuis JD.Fasting as a metabolic stress paradigm selectively amplifies cortisol

secretory burst mass and delays the time of maximal nyctohemeral cortisol concentrations in healthy men. *J Clin Endocrinol Metab.* 1996 Feb;81(2):692-9.

[106] Soeters MR. Intermittent fasting does not affect whole-body glucose, lipid, or protein metabolism. *American Journal of Clinical Nutrition.* 2009;90:1244–51.

[107] Schteingart DE, Gregerman RI, Conn JW. A comparison of the characteristics of increased adrenocortical function in obesity and Cushing's Syndrome. *Metabolism* 1963;1:261-85.

[108] Morton NM. Obesity and corticosteroids: 11beta-hydroxysteroid type 1 as a cause and therapeutic target in metabolic disease. *Mol Cell Endocrinol* 2010;316:154-164.

[109] Jacoangeli F, Zoli A, Taranto A, et al. Osteoporosis and anorexia nervosa: relative role of endocrine alterations and malnutrition. *Eat Weight Disord* 2002;7:190-195.

[110] Guthrie HA. Introductory nutrition. 6th ed. St Louis Times Mirror/ Mosby College Publishing, 1986.

[111] Song WO, Chun OK, Obayashi S, Cho S, Chung CE. Is consumption of breakfast associated with body mass index in US adults? *J Am Diet Assoc* 2005;105(9):1373-82.

[112] Gibson SA, O'Sullivan KR: Breakfast cereal consumption patterns and nutrient intakes of British school children. *J R Soc Health* 1995;115:336–370.

[113] Shlundt DG, Hill JO, Sbrocco T, Pope-Cordle J, Sharp T. The role of breakfast in the treatment of obesity: A randomized clinical trial. *Am J Clin Nutr* 1992;55:645-51.

[114] Cotton JR, Burley VJ, Blundell JE. Fat and satiety: No additional intensification of satiety following a fat supplement breakfast. *Int J Obes,*1992;16(suppl 1):11.

[115] Cotton JR, Burley VJ, Blundell JE: Fat and satiety - effect of fat in combination with either protein or carbohydrate. *Obesity and Europe.* Volume 93. London: J. Libbey; 1994:349-355.

[116] Shlundt DG, Hill JO, Sbrocco T, Pope-Cordle J, Sharp T. The role of breakfast in the treatment of obesity: A randomized clinical trial. *Am J Clin Nutr* 1992;55:645-51.

[117] Morgan KJ, Zabik ME, Stampley GL. The role of breakfast in the diet adequacy of the U.S. adult population. *J Am Coil Nutr* l986;5:551-63.

[118] Martin A, Normand S, Sothier M, Peyrat J, Louche-Pelissier C, Laville M. Is advice for breakfast consumption justified? Results from a short-term dietary and metabolic experiment in young healthy men. *British Journal of Nutrition* 2000;8:337-344.

119 Shlundt DG, Hill JO, Sbrocco T, Pope-Cordle J, Sharp T. The role of breakfast in the treatment of obesity: A randomized clinical trial. *Am J Clin Nutr* 1992;55:645-51.

120 Sarri KO, et al. Greek Orthodox fasting rituals: a hidden characteristic of the Mediterranean diet of Crete. *British Journal of Nutrition.* 2004;92:277-284.

121 Sarri KO, et al. Effects of Greek Orthodox Christian Church fasting on serum lipids and obesity. *BMC Public Health.* 2003;3:3-16.

122 Neel JV. Diabetes Mellitus: A "thrifty" genotype rendered detrimental by progress? *The American Journal of Human Genetics.* 1962;14:353-362.

123 Randle PJ, Garland PB, Hales CN, Newsholme EA, The glucose fatty-acid cycle. Its role in insulin sensitivity and the metabolic disturbances of diabetes mellitus. *Lancet* 1963;1:785-789.

124 Rabinowitz D, Zierler KL. A metabolic regulating device based on the actions of growth hormone and of insulin singly and together in the human forearm. *Nature* 1963;199:913-915.

125 Halberg N, et al. Effect of intermittent fasting and refeeding on insulin action in healthy men. *Journal of Applied Physiology* 2005;99:2128-2136.

126 Klein S, et al. Progressive Alterations in lipid and glucose metabolism during short-term fasting in young adult men. *American Journal of Physiology* 1993;265 (Endocrinology and metabolism 28):E801-E806.

127 Soules MR, Merriggiola MC, Steiner RA, Clifton DK, Toivola B, Bremner WJ. Short-Term fasting in normal women: absence of effects on gonadotrophin secretion and the menstrual cycle. *Clinical Endocrinology* 1994;40:725-731.

128 Hosker J, Matthews D, Rudenski A, Burnett M, Darling P, Bown E, Turner R: Continuous infusion of glucose with model assessment: measurement of insulin resistance and b-cell function in man. *Diabetologia* 1985;28:401–411.

129 Turner R, Holman R, Matthews D, Hockaday T, Peto J: Insulin deficiency and insulin resistance interaction in diabetes: estimation of their relative contribution by feedback analysis from basal plasma insulin and glucose concentrations. *Metabolism* 1979;28:1086–1096.

130 Matthews D, Hosker J, Rudenski A, Naylor B, Treacher D, Turner R. Homeostasis model assessment: insulin resistance and b-cell function from fasting plasma glucose and insulin concentrations in man. *Diabetologia* 1985;28:412–419.

131 Wong MH, Holst C, Astrup A, Handjieva-Darlenska T, Jebb SA, Kafatos A, Kunesova M, Larsen TM, Martinez JA, Pfeiffer AF, van Baak MA, Saris WH, McNicholas PD, Mutch DM; DiOGenes. Caloric

restriction induces changes in insulin and body weight measurements that are inversely associated with subsequent weight regain. *PLoS One.* 2012;7(8):e42858.

132 Svendsen PF, Jensen FK, Holst JJ, Haugaard SB, Nilas L, Madsbad S. The effect of a very low calorie diet on insulin sensitivity, beta cell function, insulin clearance, incretin hormone secretion, androgen levels and body composition in obese young women.*Scand J Clin Lab Invest.* 2012 Sep;72(5):410-9.

133 Mason C, Foster-Schubert KE, Imayama I, Kong A, Xiao L, Bain C, Campbell KL, Wang CY, Duggan CR, Ulrich CM, Alfano CM, Blackburn GL, McTiernan A. Dietary weight loss and exercise effects on insulin resistance in postmenopausal women. *Am J Prev Med.* 2011 Oct;41(4):366-75.

134 Kassi E, Papavassiliou AG. Could glucose be a pro-aging factor? *Journal of Cellular and Molecular medicine.* 2008;12(4):1194-8.

135 Ling PR, Smith RJ, Bistrian BR. Acute effects of hyperglycemia and hyperinsulinemia on hepatic oxidative stress and the systemic inflammatory response in rats. *Critical Care Medicine* 2007;35:555-560.

136 Klein S, et al. Progressive Alterations in lipid and glucose metabolism during short-term fasting in young adult men. *American Journal of Physiology* 1993;265 (Endocrinology and metabolism 28):E801-E806.

137 Zechner R, Kienseberger PC, Hammerle G, Zimmermann R, Lass A. Adipose triglyceride lipase and the lipolytic catabolism of cellular fat stores. *Journal of Lipid Research* 2009;50:3-21.

138 Nielsen TS, Vandelbo MH, Jessen N, Pedersen SB, Jorgensen JO, Lund S, Moller N. Fasting, but not exercise, increases adipose triglyceride lipase (ATGL) protein and reduces G(0)/G(1) switch gene 2 (G0S2) protein and mRNA content in human adipose tissue. *J Clin Endocrin Metab.* 2011;96:E0000-E0000.

139 Tunstall RJ, et al. Fasting activates the gene expression of UCP3 independent of genes necessary for lipid transport and oxidation in skeletal muscle. *Biochemical and Biophysical Research Communications* 2002;294:301-308.

140 Eakman GD, Dallas JS, Ponder SW, Keenan BS. The effects of testosterone and dihydrotestosterone on hypothalamic regulation of growth hormone secretion. *J Clin Endocrinol Metab 1996;* 81:1217–1223.

141 Lang I, Schernthaner G, Pietschmann P, Kurz R, Stephenson JM, Templ H. Effects of sex and age on growth hormone response to growth hormone-releasing hormone in healthy individuals. *J Clin Endocrinol Metab 1987;* 65:535–540.

142 Aragon-Vargas LF. Effects of fasting on endurance exercise. *Sports Med* 1993;16:255-65.

143 Hartman ML, et al. Augmented growth hormone (GH) secretory burst frequency and amplitude mediate enhanced CH secretion during a two-day fast in normal men. *Journal of Clinical Endocrinology and Metabolism* 1992;74(4):757-765.

144 Vendelbo MH, Jorgensen JO, Pedersen SB, Gormsen LC, Lund S, Schmitz O, Jessen N, and Moller N. Exercise and fasting activate growth hormone-dependent myocellular signal transducer and Activator of transcription-5b phosphorylation and Insulin-like growth factor-1 messenger ribonucleic acid expression in humans. *Journal of Clinical Endocrinology and Metabolism.* 2010;95(9):1-5.

145 Rizza RA, Mandarino LJ & Gerich JE. Effects of growth hormone on insulin action in man. Mechanism of insulin resistance, impaired suppression of glucose production, and impaired stimulation of glucose utilization. *Diabetes* 1982;31:663–669.

146 Norrelund H. Modulation of basal glucose metabolism and insulin sensitivity by growth hormone and free fatty acids during short-term fasting. *European Journal of Endocrinology* 2004;150:779-787.

147 Hansen M, et al. Effects of 2 wk of GH administration on 24-h indirect calorimetry in young, healthy, lean men. American *Journal of Physiology Endocrinology and Metabolism* 2005;289:E1030-E1038

148 Moller L, Dalman L, Norrelund H, Billestrup N, Frystyk J, Moller N, and Jorgensen JOL. Impact of fasting on growth hormone signaling and action in muscle and fat. *Journal of Clinical Endocrinology and Metabolism.* 2009;4:965-972.

149 Szego CM, White A. The influence of purified growth hormone on fasting metabolism. *J Clin Endocrinol Metab* 8;1948:594.

150 Norrelund H. The protein-retaining effects of growth hormone during fasting involve inhibition of muscle- protein breakdown. *Diabetes* 2001;50:96-104.

151 Norrelund H, Rils AL, Moller N. Effects of GH on protein metabolism during dietary restriction in man. *Growth hormone & IGF Research* 2002;12:198-207.

152 Moller N, Jorgensen JO. Effects of growth hormone on glucose, lipid and protein metabolism in human subjects. *Endocrine Reviews.* 2009;30:152-177.

153 Norrelund H. Abstracts of Ph.D. dissertation – effects of growth hormone on protein metabolism during dietary restriction. Studies in normal, GH-deficient and obese subjects. *Danish Medical Bulletin* 2001;47(5):370.

154 Norrelund H. The metabolic role of growth hormone in humans with particular reference to fasting. *Growth Hormone and IGF research.* 2005;15:95-122.

155 Oscarsson J, Ottosson M, Eden S. Effects of growth hormone on lipoprotein lipase and hepatic lipase. *J Endocrinol Invest* 1999;22:2-9.

156 Oscarsson J, Ottosson M, Vikman-adolfsson K, et al. GH but not IGF-1 or insulin increases lipoprotein lipase activity in muscle tissues of hypophysectomised rats. *J Endocrinol.* 1999;160:247-255.

157 Veldhuis JD, Iranmanesh A, Ho KK, Waters MJ, Johnson ML, Lizarralde G. Dual defects in pulsatile growth hormone secretion and clearance subserve the hyposomatotropism of obesity in man. *J Clin Endocrinol Metab.* 1991 Jan;72(1):51-9.

158 Cornford AS, Barkan AL, Horowitz JF. Rapid suppression of Growth Hormone concentration by overeating: Potential mediation by hyperinsulinemia. *J Clin Endocrinol Metab* 2011;96:824-830.

159 Rabinowitz D, Zierler KL. A metabolic regulating device based on the actions of growth hormone and of insulin singly and together in the human forearm. *Nature* 1963;199:913-915.

160 Rabinowitz D, Zierler KL. A metabolic regulating device based on the actions of growth hormone and of insulin singly and together in the human forearm. *Nature* 1963;199:913-915.

161 Veldhuis JD, Roemmich JN, Richmond EJ, Bowers CY. Somatotropic and gonadotropic axes linkages in infancy, childhood, and the puberty adult transition. *Endocr Rev* 2006;27:101–140.

162 Veldhuis JD. Aging and hormones of the hypothalamo-pituitary axis: gonadotropic axis in men and somatotropic axes in men and women. *Aging Research Reviews.* 2008;7:189–208.

163 Finkelstein JW, Roffwarg HP, Boyar RM, Kream J, Hellman L. Age-related change in the twenty-four- hour spontaneous secretion of growth hormone. *Journal of Clinical Endocrinology and Metabolism.* 1972 Nov;35(5):665-70.

164 Corpas E, Harman SM, Blackman MR. Human growth hormone and human aging. *Endocrine Reviews.* 1993;14:20–39.

165 Frayne, K.N. Insulin resistance and lipid metabolism. *Curr. Opin. Lipidol.* 1993;4:197–204.

166 Boden, G., Chen, X., Ruiz, J., White, J.V., and Rosetti, L. Mechanism of fatty acid induced inhibition of glucose uptake. *J. Clin. Invest.* 1994; 93:2438–2446.

167 Moller L, Dalman L, Norrelund H, Billestrup N, Frystyk J, Moller N, and Jorgensen JOL. Impact of fasting on growth hormone signaling and action in muscle and fat. *Journal of Clinical Endocrinology and Metabolism.* 2009;4:965-972.

168 Kanaley JA, Weatherup-Dentes MM, Jaynes EB, Hartman ML. Obesity attenuates the growth hormone response to exercise. *Journal of Clinical Endocrinology Metabolism*. 1999;84:3156-3161.

169 Redman LM, Veldhuis JD, Rood J, Smith SR, Williamson D, Ravussin E; Pennington CALERIE Team. The effect of caloric restriction interventions on growth hormone secretion in nonobese men and women. *Aging Cell*. 2010 Feb;9(1):32-9.

170 Rasmussen MH, Hvidberg A, Juul A, et al. Massive weight loss restores 24-hour growth hormone release profiles and serum insulin-like growth factor-I levels in obese subjects. *Journal of Clinical Endocrinology Metabolism*. 1999;80:1407-1415.

171 Mauras N, O'brien KO, Welch S, et al. Insulin-like growth factor 1 and growth hormone (GH) treatment   in GH-Deficient humans: differential effects on protein, glucose, lipid and calcium metabolism. *J Clin Endocrinol Metab* 2000;85:1686-1694.

172 Rennie MJ. Claims for the anabolic effects of growth hormone: a case of the Emperor's new clothes? *British Journal of Sports Medicine* 2003;37:100–105.

173 Wansink, Brian. *Marketing Food*. Champaign, Illinois: University of Illinois Press. 2005.

174 Duncan GG, Cristofori FC, Yue JK, Murthy MSJ: Control of obesity by intermittent fasts. *Med Clin N Amer* 1964;48:1359.

175 Johnstone, AM. Fasting–the ultimate diet? *Obesity Reviews* 2007;8(3):211-222.

176 Lionetti L, Mollica MP, Lombardi A, Cavaliere G, Gifuni G, Barletta A. From chronic overnutrition to insulin resistance: The role of fat-storing capacity and inflammation. Nutrition, *Metabolism & Cardiovascular Disease* 2009;19:146-152.

177 Chung HY, Kim HJ, Kim JW, Yu BP. The inflammation hypothesis of aging: molecular modulation by calorie restriction. *Annals of the New York Academy of Sciences*. 2001;928:327-35.

178 Senn JJ, Klover PJ, Nowak IA, and Moony RA. IL-6 induces cellular insulin resistance in hepatocytes. *Diabetes*. 2002;51(12):3391-9.

179 Bharat B. Aggarwal, R.V. Vijayalekshmi, and Bokyung Sung. Targeting inflammatory pathways for prevention and therapy of cancer: Short-term friend, long-term foe. *Clinical Cancer Research* 2009;15(2):425-430.

180 Kershaw EE, Flier JS. Adipose tissue as an endocrine organ. *Journal of Clinical Endocrinology and Metabolism*. 2004; 89:2548–2556.

181 Loffreda S, Yang SQ, Lin HZ, Karp CL, Brengman ML, Wang DJ, Klein AS, Bulkley GB, Bao C, Noble PW, Lane MD, Diehl AM. Leptin

regulates proinflammatory immune responses. *Federation of American Societies for Experimental Biology Journal*. 1998 Jan;12(1):57-65.

[182] Esposito K, Nappo F, Marfella R, Giugliano G, Giugliano F, Ciotola M, Quagliaro L, Ceriello A, Giugliano D. Inflammatory cytokine concentrations are acutely increased by hyperglycemia in humans: Role of oxidative stress. *Circulation*. 2002 Oct 15;106(16):2067-72.

[183] Dixit VD. Adipose-immune interactions during obesity and caloric restriction: Reciprocal mechanisms regulating immunity and health span. *Journal of Leukocyte Biology*. 2008;84:882-892.

[184] Morgan TE, Wong AM, and Finch CE. Anti-inflammatory mechanisms of dietary restriction in slowing aging processes. *Interdisciplinary Topics in Gerontology*. 2007;35:83-97.

[185] Fontana L. Neuroendocrine factors in the regulations of inflammation: Excessive adiposity and caloric restriction. *Experimental Gerontology*. 2009;44:41-45.

[186] Prestes J, Shiguemoto G, Botero JP, Frollini A, Dias R, Leite R, et al. Effects of resistance training on resistin, leptin, cytokines, and muscle force in elderly post-menopausal women. *Journal of Sports Science*. 2009;27(14):1607-1615.

[187] Bruun JM, Helge JW, Richelsen B, Stallknecht B. Diet and exercise reduce low-grade inflammation and macrophage infiltration in adipose tissue but not in skeletal muscle in severely obese subjects. *American Journal of Physiology Endocrinology and Metabolism*. 2006 May;290(5):E961-7.

[188] Schapp LA, Plijm SMF, Deeg DJh and Visser M. Inflammatory markers and loss of muscle mass (sarcopenia) and strength. *American Journal of Medicine*. 2006;199:U82-U90.

[189] Toth MH, Matthews DE, Tracy RP and Previs MJ. Age-related differences in skeletal muscle protein synthesis: Relation to markers of immune activation. *American Journal of Physiology Endocrinology and Metabolism* 2005;288:E883-E891.

[190] Visser M, Pahor M, Taaffe DR, Goodpaster BH, Simonsick EM, Newman AB et al. Relationship of interluekin-6 and tumor necrosis factor-α with muscle mass and muscle strength in elderly men and women. The health ABC study. *Journal of Gerontology Series A: Biological Science and Medical Science* 2002;57:M326-M332.

[191] Deter RL, De Duve C. Influence of glucagon, an inducer of cellular autophagy, on some physical properties of rat liver lysosomes. *J Cell Biol* 1967;33:437–449

[192] A.M. Cuervo, E. Bergamini, U.T. Brunk, W. Droge, M. Ffrench, A. Terman, Autophagy and aging: The importance of maintaining "clean" cells, *Autophagy* 1 2005;131e140.

193 T Kanazawa, Ikue Taneike, Ryuichiro Akaishi, Fumiaki Yoshizawa, Norihiko Furuya, Shinobu Fujimura, and Motoni Kadowaki. Amino acids and insulin control autophagic proteolysis through different signaling pathways in relation to mTOR in isolated rat hepatocytes. *The Journal of Biological Chemistry.* 2004 Feb 27;279(9):8452–8459

194 Glynn EL, Fry CS, Drummond MJ, Timmerman KL, Dhanani S, Volpi E, Rasmussen BB. Excess leucine intake enhances muscle anabolic signaling but not net protein anabolism in young men and women. *J Nutr.* 2010 Nov;140(11):1970-6.

195 Joon-Ho Sheen, Roberto Zoncu, Dohoon Kim, David M. Sabatini defective regulation of autophagy upon leucine deprivation reveals a targetable liability of human melanoma cells in vitro and in vivo. *Cancer Cell.* 2011 May 17;19(5):613-628.

196 Ding, WX. The emerging role of autophagy in alcoholic liver disease *Exp Biol Med* 1 May 2011;546-556.

197 Hara T, et al. Suppression of basal autophagy in neural cells causes neurodegenerative disease in mice. *Nature* 2006;441:885-9.

198 Komatsu M, et al. Loss of autophagy in the central nervous system causes neurodegeneration in mice. *Nature* 2006;441:880-4.

199 Mizushima N, Levine B, Cuervo AM, Klionsky DJ. Autophagy fights disease through cellular self- digestion. *Nature* 2008;451:1069-75.

200 Alirezaei M, Kiosses WB, Flynn CT, Brady NR, Fox HS. Disruption of neuronal autophagy by infected microglia results in neurodegeneration. *PLoS ONE* 2008;3:2906.

201 Orvedahl A, Levine B. Eating the enemy within: Autophagy in infectious diseases. *Cell Death Differ* 2009; 16:57-69.

202 Alirezaei M, Kemball CC, Flynn CT, Wood MR, Whitton JL, Kiosses WB. Short-term fasting induces profound neuronal autophagy. *Autophagy.* 2010 Aug;6(6):702-10.

203 Hara, N., K. Nakamura, M. Matsui, A. Yamamoto, Y. Nakahara, R. Suzuki-Migishima, M. Yokoyama, K. Mishima, I. Saito, H. Okana, and N. Mizushima. Suppression of basal autophagy in neural cells causes neurodegenerative disease in mice. *Nature.* 2006 June 15;441(7095)885-9.

204 Komatsu M, et al. Loss of autophagy in the central nervous system causes neurodegeneration in mice. *Nature* 2006;441:880-4.

205 Jaeger PA, Wyss-Coray T. All-you-can-eat: Autophagy in neurodegeneration and neuroprotection. *Mol Neurodegener* 2009;4:16.

206 Hung SY, Huang WP, Liou HC, Fu WM. Autophagy protects neuron from abeta-induced cytotoxicity. *Autophagy* 2009;5:502-10.

207 Donati A, Cavallini G., Paradiso C., Vittorini S., Pollera M., Gori Z. and E. B. Age-related changes in the autophagic proteolysis of rat isolated liver cells: Effects of antiaging dietary restrictions. *J Gerontol A Biol Sci Med* Sci. 2001;56:B375-383.

208 Rubinsztein DC. The roles of intracellular protein-degradation pathways in neurodegeneration. *Nature*. 2006;443:780-786.

209 K. Kirkegaard, M.P. Taylor, W.T. Jackson, Cellular autophagy: Surrender, avoidance and subversion by microorganisms. *Nat. Rev. Microbiol.* 2 2004;301-314.

210 B. Levine, Eating oneself and uninvited guests: Autophagy-related pathways in cellular defense. *Cell* 2005;120:159-162.

211 M. Ogawa, C. Sasakawa, Bacterial evasion of the autophagic defense system. *Curr. Opin. Microbiol.* 2006;9:62-68.

212 M.S. Swanson, Autophagy: Eating for good health. *J Immunol.* 2006;177:4945-4951.

213 Anson RM, et al. Intermittent fasting dissociates beneficial effects of dietary restriction on glucose metabolism and neuronal resistance to injury from calorie intake. *Proc Natl Acad Sci USA* 2003;100:6216- 20.

214 Duan W, et al. Dietary restriction normalizes glucose metabolism and BDNF levels, slows disease progression, and increases survival in hunting mutant mice. *Proc Natl Acad Sci USA* 2003;100:2911-6.

215 Tohyama D, Yamaguchi A and Yamashita T. Inhibition of a eukaryotic initiation factor (eIF2Bdelta/F11A3.2) during adulthood extends lifespan in caenorhabditis elegans. *FASEB J.* 2008;22: 4327-4337.

216 Nair U, Klionsky DJ. Activation of autophagy is required for muscle homeostasis during physical exercise. *Autophagy.* 2011;Dec1;7(12).

217 Sandri M. Autophagy in health and disease. 3. Involvement of autophagy in muscle atrophy. *Am J Physiol Cell Physiol* 2010;298:C1291-7.

218 Drummond DA. Mistranslation-induced protein misfolding as a dominant constraint on coding-sequence evolution. *Cell.* 2008;134:341-352.

219 Fishebin L, *Biological effects of Dietary Restriction.* New York: Springer-Verlag, 1991.

220 Lane MA, Ingram DK, Roth GS. Caloric restriction in nonhuman primates: Effects on diabetes and cardiovascular disease risk. *Toxilogical Sciences* 1999;52s:41-48.

221 Varaday KA, Bhutani S, Church EC, Klempel EC, Short-term modified alternate-day fasting: A novel dietary strategy for weight loss and cardioprotection in obese adults. *American Journal of Clinical Nutrition* 2009;90:1138–43.

222 Nestle, Marion. *Food politics*. Los Angeles, California: University of California Press. 2003.

223 Stirling LJ, Yeomans MR. Effect of exposure to a forbidden food on eating in restrained and unrestrained women. *Int J Eat Disord* 2004;35:59–68.

224 Rogers PJ, Smit HJ. Food craving and food "addiction": A critical review of the evidence from a biopsychosocial perspective. *Pharmacology Biochemistry and Behavior*. 2000;66(1):3–14.

225 Bernard, C. *Lecon de Physiologie Expdrirnentale Appliqute ci la Midecine. faites au College de France. Tome IeTC: ours du semester d'hiver 1854-1855*. J.-B. BailliBre, Paris, 1855.

226 Randle PJ, Garland PB, Hales CN, and Newsholme EA. The glucose fatty-acid cycle. Its role in insulin sensitivity and the metabolic disturbances of diabetes mellitus. *Lancet 1963*; 1:785-789.

227 Vendelbo MH, Clasen BF, Treebak JT, Møller L, Krusenstjerna-Hafstrøm T, Madsen M, Nielsen TS, Stødkilde-Jørgensen H, Pedersen SB, Jørgensen JO, Goodyear LJ, Wojtaszewski JF, Møller N, Jessen N. Insulin resistance after a 72-h fast is associated with impaired AS160 phosphorylation and accumulation of lipid and glycogen in human skeletal muscle. *Am J Physiol Endocrinol Metab* 2012;302:E190– E200.

228 Nilsson LH, and Hultman E. Liver glycogen in man--the effect of total starvation or a carbohydrate-poor diet followed by carbohydrate refeeding. *Scand J Clin Lab Invest 1973*; 32:325-330.

229 Green JG, Johnson NA, Sachinwalla T, Cunningham CW, Thompson MW, Stannard SR. Moderate- intensity endurance exercise prevents short-term starvation-induced intramyocellular lipid accumulation but not insulin resistance. *Metabolism 2011*; 60:1051–1057.

230 Johnson NA, Stannard SR, Rowlands DS, Chapman PG, Thompson CH, O'Connor H, Sachinwalla T, Thompson MW. Effect of short-term starvation versus high-fat diet on intramyocellular triglyceride accumulation and insulin resistance in physically fit men. *Exp Physiol 2006*; 91:693–703.

231 Bergman BC, Cornier MA, Horton TJ, Bessesen DH. Effects of fasting on insulin action and glucose kinetics in lean and obese men and women. *Am J Physiol Endocrinol Metab 2007*; 293:E1103–E1111.

232 Bergman BC, Cornier MA, Horton TJ, Bessesen DH. Effects of fasting on insulin action and glucose kinetics in lean and obese men and women. *Am J Physiol Endocrinol Metab 2007*; 293:E1103–E1111.

233 Dominici FP, Argentino DP, Bartke A, Turyn D. The dwarf mutation decreases high dose insulin responses in skeletal muscle, the opposite of effects in liver. *Mech Aging Dev* 2003;124:819–827.

[234] Salih DA, Brunet A. FoxO transcription factors in the maintenance of cellular homeostasis during aging. *Curr Opin Cell Biol* 2008; 20:126–136.

[235] Albala, K. *Food in Early Modern Europe*. Westport, CT: Greenwood Press, 2003; 232.

[236] Visser, M. *Rituals of Dinner*. New York: Penguin, 1991;158-9.

[237] Herman CP, Mack D. Restrained and unrestrained eating. *Journal of Personality*. 1975;43:647-660.

[238] Herman CP, Polivy J. The self-regulation of eating. *Journal of Personality* 1992;43:647-660.

[239] Knight LJ, Boland FJ. Restrained eating: An experimental disentanglement of the disinhibiting variables of perceived calories and food type. *Journal of Abnormal psychology* 1989;98;412-420.

[240] Westenhoefer J, Stunkard AJ, Pudel V. Validation of the flexible and rigid control dimensions of dietary restraint. *International journal of Eating Disorders* 1999;26:53-64.

[241] Wansink, Brian. *Mindless Eating*. New York: Bantam Dell (A division of Random House, Inc.) 2006.

[242] Halberg N, Henriksen M, Soderhamn N, et al. Effect of intermittent fasting and refeeding on insulin action healthy men. *Journal of Applied Physiology* 2005; 99:2128-2136.

[243] Carlson HE, Shah JH. Aspartame and its constituent amino acids: Effects on prolactin, cortisol, growth hormone, insulin, and glucose in normal humans. *American Journal of Clinical Nutrition*. 1989:49;427-32.

[244] Okuno G, Kawakami F, Tako H, Kashihara T, Shibamoto S, Yamazaki T, Yamamoto K, Saeki M. Glucose tolerance, blood lipid, insulin and glucagon concentration after single or continuous administration of aspartame in diabetics. *Diabetes Research and Clinical Practice* 1986 Apr;2(1):23-7.

[245] Petrie HJ, Chown SE, Belfie LM, Duncan AM, McLaren DH, Conquer JA, Graham TE. Caffeine ingestion increases the insulin response to an oral-glucose-tolerance test in obese men before and after weight loss. *American Journal of Clinical Nutrition*. 2004 Jul;80(1):22-8.

[246] Graham TE, Sathasivam P, Rowland M, Marko N, Greer F, Battram D. Caffeine ingestion elevates plasma insulin response in humans during an oral glucose tolerance test. *Canadian Journal of Physiology and Pharmacology* 2001 Jul;79(7):559-65.

[247] Ho KY, Evans WS, Blizzard RM, Veldhuis JD, Merriam GR, Samojlik E, Furlanetto R, Rogol AD, Kaiser DL, Thorner MO. Effects of sex and age on the 24-hour profile of growth hormone secretion in man: Importance of endogenous estradiol concentrations. *J Clin Endocrinol Metab* 1987;64:51–58.

248 Yen SSC, Vela P, Rankin J, Littell AS. Hormonal relationships during the menstrual cycle. *JAMA*. 1970;211:1513–1517.

249 Devesa J, Lois N, Arce V, Diaz MJ, Lima L, Tresguerres JA. The role of sexual steroids in the modulation of growth hormone (GH) secretion in humans. *J Steroid Biochem Mol Biol*. 1991;40:165–173.

250 Veldhuis J.D. et al. Relative effects of estrogen, age, and visceral fat on pulsatile growth hormone secretion in healthy women. *Am J Physiol Endocrinol Metab* 2009;297: E367-E74.

251 Weltman A, Weltman JY, Hartman ML, et al. Relationship between age, percentage body fat, fitness and 24-hour growth hormone release in healthy young adults: Effects of gender. *J Clin Endocrinol Metab*. 1994;78:543–548.

252 Wennink JMB, Delemarre-van de Waal HA, Schoemaker R, Blaauw G, van den Brakern C, Schoemaker J. Growth hormone secretion patterns in relation to LH and estradiol secretion throughout normal female puberty. *ActaEndocrinol* (Copenh). 1991;124:129–135.

253 Frantz AG, Rabkin MT. Effects of estrogen and sex difference on secretion of human growth hormone. *J Clin Endocrinol Metab*. 1965;25:1470 –1480.

254 Merimee TJ, Fineberg SE. Studies of the sex-based variation of human growth hormone secretion. *J Clin Endocrinol Metab*. 1971;33:896 –902.

255 Heilbronn LK, Civitarese AE, Bogacka I, Smith ST, Hulver M, Ravussin E. Glucose tolerance and skeletal muscle gene expression in response to alternate day fasting. *Obse Res*. 2005;13:574-581.

256 Warren MP, Vande Wiele RL. Clinical and metabolic features of anorexia nervosa. *Am J Obstet Gynecol*. 1973;117:435–449.

257 Frisch RE, Wyshak G, Vincent L. Delayed menarche and amenorrhea in ballet dancers. *N Engl J Med*. 1980;303:17–19.

258 Frisch, RE, McArthur. Menstrual cycles: Fatness as a determinant of minimum weight for height necessary for their maintenance or onset. *Science*. 1974;185:949

259 Friedl KE, et al. Lower limit of body fat in healthy active men. *J Appl Physiol*. 1994;77(2):933-940.

260 Thong, FSL, McLean C, Graham TE. Plasma leptin in female athletes: Relationship with body fat, reproductive, nutritional, and endocrine factors. *J Appl Physiol*. 2000;88:2037–2044.

261 Azizi F. Effect of dietary composition on fasting-induced changes in serum thyroid hormones and thyrotropin. *Metabolism*.1978 Aug;27(8)935-42.

262 Borissova AM, Tankova T, Kirilov G, Koev D. Gender-dependent effect of aging on peripheral insulin action. *Int J Clin Pract* 2005;59:422–426.

263 Paula FJ, Pimenta WP, Saad MJ, Paccola GM, Piccinato CE, Foss MC. Sex-related differences in peripheral glucose metabolism in normal subjects. *Diabetes Metab* 1990;16:234–239.

264 Soeters MR, Sauerwein HP, Groener JE, Aerts JM, Ackermans MT, Glatz JF, Fliers E, Serlie MJ.Gender- related differences in the metabolic response to fasting. *J Clin Endocrinol Metab.* 2007 Sep;92(9):3646-52. Epub 2007Jun;12.

265 Bergman BC, Cornier M-A, Horton TJ, Bessesen DH. Effects of fasting on insulin action and glucose kinetics in lean and obese men and women. *Am J Physiol Endocrinol Metab* 2007;293:E1103–E1111.

266 Lado-Abeal J, Prieto D, Lorenzo M, Lojo S, Febrero M, Camarero E, Cabezas-Cerrato J. Differences between men and women as regards the effects of protein-energy malnutrition on the hypothalamic-pituitary-gonadal axis. *Nutrition.* 1999 May;15(5):351-8.

267 Mittendorfer B, Horowitz JF, Klein S. Gender differences in lipid and glucose kinetics during short-term fasting. *Am J Physiol Endocrinol Metab* 2001;281:E1333–E1339.

268 Soeters MR, Sauerwein HP, Groener JE, Aerts JM, Ackermans MT, Glatz JF, Fliers E, Serlie MJ. Gender- related differences in the metabolic response to fasting. *J Clin Endocrinol Metab* 2007;92: 3646–3652.

269 Kiens , B, Roepstorff C , Glatz, JF, Bonen, A , Schjerling, P, Knudsen, J, and Nielsen, JN. Lipid-binding proteins and lipoprotein lipase activity in human skeletal muscle: Influence of physical activity and gender. *J. Appl. Physiol.* 2004;97:1209–1218.

270 Klempel MC, Kroeger CM, Bhutani S, Trepanowski JF, Varady KA.Intermittent fasting combined with calorie restriction is effective for weight loss and cardio-protection in obese women.*Nutr J.* 2012 Nov 21;11:98.

271 Harvie MN, Pegington M, Mattson MP, Frystyk J, Dillon B, Evans G, Cuzick J, Jebb SA, Martin B, Cutler RG, Son TG, Maudsley S, Carlson OD, Egan JM, Flyvbjerg A, Howell A.The effects of intermittent or continuous energy restriction on weight loss and metabolic disease risk markers: A randomized trial in young overweight women. *Int J Obes* (Lond). 2011 May;35(5):714-27.

272 Data tabulated from *VenusIndex.com*

273 Exercise AC. Ace Lifestyle & Weight Management Consultant Manual, The Ultimate Resource for Fitness Professionals. *American Council on Exercise*; 2009.

274 Alvero R, Kimzey L, Sebring N, Reynolds J, Loughran M, Nieman L, Olson BR.Effects of fasting on neuroendocrine function and follicle development in lean women. *J Clin Endocrinol Metab.* 1998 Jan;83(1):76-80.

275 Olson BR, Cartledge T, Sebring N, Defensor R, Nieman L. Short-term fasting affects luteinizing hormone secretory dynamics but not reproductive function in normal-weight sedentary women. *J Clin Endocrinol Metab*. 1995;80:1187–1193.

276 Klibanski A, Beitins IZ, Badger T, Little R, McArthur JW. Reproductive function during fasting in men. *J Clin Endocrinol Metab. 1981 Aug;53(2):258-63.*

277 Friedl KE et al. Endocrine markers of semistarvation in healthy lean men in a multistressor environment. *J Appl Physiol* 2000;88:1820-1830.

278 Dye L, Blundell JE. Menstrual cycle and appetite control: Implications for weight regulation. *Hum Reprod* 1997;12:1142-51.

279 Van Vugt DA. Brain imaging studies of appetite in the context of obesity and the menstrual cycle. *Hum Reprod* Update 2010;16:276–92.

280 Asarian L, Geary N. Modulation of appetite by gonadal steroid hormones. *Philos Trans R Soc Lond B Biol Sci* 2006;361:1251–63.

281 Alonso-Alonso M, Ziemke F, Magkos F, Barrios FA, e al. Brain responses to food images during the early and late follicular phase of the menstrual cycle in healthy young women: Relation to fasting and feeding. *Am J Clin Nutr*. 2011 Aug;94(2):377-84.

282 Goldberg AL, Etlinger JD, Goldspink DF, Jablecki C. Mechanism of work-induced hypertrophy of skeletal muscle. *Medicine and Science in Sports Exercise*. 1975;7:248-61.

283 Bean J, Frontera W. *Strength and Power Training*. Harvard Health Publications. 2008.

284 Hausenblas HA, Falloon EA. Exercise and body image: A meta analysis. *Psychology and health*. 2006; 21:33-47.

285 Wernbom M, Augustsson J, Thome´e R. The Influence of frequency, intensity, volume and mode of strength training on whole muscle cross-sectional area in humans. *Sports Medicine* 2007; 37(3):225-264.

286 Burd NA, West DWD, Staples AW, et al. Low-load high volume resistance exercise stimulates muscle protein synthesis more than high-load low volume resistance exercise in young men. *Plos One* 2010; 5(8): e12033.

287 Dishman RK. *Exercise Adherence: Its Impact on Public Health*. Champaign, Il: Human Kinetics, 1988.

288 Niven A, Rendell E, Chisholm L. Effects of 72-h of exercise abstinence on affect and body dissatisfaction in healthy female regular exercisers. *Journal of Sports Sciences* 2008; 26(11):1235-1242.

289 Benjamin R. The Surgeon General's Vision for a Healthy and Fit Nation. Rockville, MD: U.S. Department of Health and Human Services, Public Health Service, Office of the Surgeon General; 2010.

290 Kiens B. Effect of endurance training on fatty acid metabolism: Local adaptations. *Med Sci Sports Exercise* 1997;29:640–645.

291 Kiens B. Effect of endurance training on fatty acid metabolism: Local adaptations. *Med Sci Sports Exercise* 1997;29:640–645.

292 Kiens B and Lithell H. Lipoprotein metabolism influenced by training-induced changes in human skeletal muscle. *J Clin Invest* 1989;83:558–564.

293 Blundell JE, Stubbs RJ, Hughes DA, Whybrow S, King NA. Cross-talk between physical activity and appetite control: Does PA stimulate appetite? *Proc Nutr Soc* 2003;62:651–661.

294 Whybrow S, Hughes DA, Ritz P, Johnstone AM, Horgan GW, King N et al. The effect of an incremental increase in exercise on appetite, eating behavior and energy balance in lean men and women feeding ad libitum. *Br J Nutr* 2008;100:1109–1115.

295 Unick JL, Otto AD, Goodpaster BH, Helsel DL, Pellegrini CA, Jakicic JM. The acute effect of walking on energy intake in overweight/obese women. *Appetite* 2010;55:413–419.

296 Pendleton VR, Goodrick GK, Poston WS, Reeves RS, Foreyt JP. Exercise augments the effects of cognitive-behavioral therapy in the treatment of binge eating. *Int J Eat Disord* 2002;31:172–84.

297 Martins C, Morgan L, Truby H. A review of the effects of exercise on appetite regulation: An obesity perspective. *Int J Obes* 2008;32:1337–1347.

298 Thompson D, Karpe F, Lafontan M, Frayn K. Physical activity and exercise in the regulation of human adipose tissue physiology. *Physiol Rev.* 2012 Jan;92(1):157-91.

299 Ismail I, Keating SE, Baker MK, Johnson NA. A systematic review and meta-analysis of the effect of aerobic vs. resistance exercise training on visceral fat. *Obes Rev.* 2012 Jan;13(1):68-91.

300 Slentz CA, Bateman LA, Willis LH, Shields AT, Tanner CJ,et al. Effects of aerobic vs. resistance training on visceral and liver fat stores, liver enzymes, and insulin resistance by HOMA in overweight adults from STRRIDE AT/RT. Am *J Physiol Endocrinol Metab.* 2011 Nov;301(5):E1033-9.

301 Jacoangeli F, Zoli A, Taranto A, et al. Osteoporosis and anorexia nervosa: Relative role of endocrine alterations and malnutrition. *Eat Weight Disord* 2002;7:190-195.

302 Henson J, Yates T, Biddle SJ, Edwardson CL, Khunti K, Wilmot EG, Gray LJ, Gorely T, Nimmo MA, Davies MJ. Associations of objectively measured sedentary behavior and physical activity with markers of cardiometabolic health. *Diabetologia.* 2013 May;56(5):1012-20.

303 Prestes J, Shiguemoto G, Botero JP, Frollini A, Dias R, Leite R, et al. Effects of resistance training on resistin, leptin, cytokines, and muscle force in elderly post-menopausal women. *Journal of Sports Science* 2009;27(14):1607-1615.

304 Bruunsgaard H. Physical activity and modulation of systemic low-level inflammation. *J Leukoc Biol* 2005;78:819-835.

305 Timmerman KL, Flynn MG, Coen PM, Markofski MM, Pence BD. Exercise training-induced lowering of inflammatory (CD14+CD16+) monocytes: A role in the anti-inflammatory influence of exercise? *Journal of Leukocyte Biology*. 2008;84:1271-1278.

306 Bean J, Frontera W. *Strength and Power Training*. Harvard Health Publications. 2008.

307 Hausenblas HA, Falloon EA. Exercise and body image: A meta analysis. *Psychology and health*. 2006. 21;33-47.

308 Ulen GC, Huizinga MM, Beecb B, Elasy TA. Weight regain prevention. *Clinical Diabetes*. 2008;26:100- 113.

309 Delbridge EA, Prendergast LA, Pritchard JE, Proietto J. One-year weight maintenance after significant weight loss in healthy overweight and obese subjects: Does diet composition matter? *American Journal of Clinical Nutrition* 2009;90:12093-13.

310 Foster GD, Wyatt HR, Hill JO, et al. A randomized trial of a low-carbohydrate diet for obesity. *New England Journal of Medicine* 2003;348:2082-90.

311 Dansinger ML, Gleason JA, Griffith JL, et al. Comparison of the Atkins, Ornish, Weight Watchers and Zone diets for weight loss and heart diseases risk reduction: A randomized trial. *Journal of the American Medical Association* 2005;293:43-53.

312 Russell J de Souza, George A Bray, Vincent J Carey, et al. Effects of 4 weight-loss diets differing in fat, protein, and carbohydrate on fat mass, lean mass, visceral adipose tissue, and hepatic fat: Results from the POUNDS LOST trial. *Am J Clin Nutr* 2012;95:614–25.

313 Vogels N, Westerterp-Plantenga MS. Successful long-term weight Maintenance: A 2-year follow up. *Obesity* 2007;15(5):1258-1266.

314 Vogels N, Westerterp-Plantenga MS. Successful long-term weight Maintenance: A 2-year follow up. *Obesity* 2007;15(5):1258-1266.

315 Westenhoefer J, Stunkard AJ, Pudel V. Validation of the flexible and rigid control dimensions of dietary restraint. *Int J Eat Disord* 1999;26:53–64.

316 Provencher V, Drapeau V, Tremblay A, Despres JP, Lemieux S. Eating behaviors and indexes of body composition in men and women from the Quebec family study. *Obes Res* 2003;11:783–92.

317 Drapeau V, Provencher V, Lemieux S, Despres JP, Bouchard C, Tremblay A. Do changes in eating behaviors predict changes in body

weight? Results from the Quebec Family Study. *Int J Obes Relat Metab Disord* 2003;27:808–14.

318 McGuire MT, Jeffery RW, French SA, Hannan PJ. The relationship between restraint and weight and weight-related behaviors among individuals in a community weight gain prevention trial. *Int J Obes Relat Metab Disord* 2001;25:574–80.

319 Provencher V, Begin C, Tremblay A, Mongeau L, Boivin S, Lemieux S. Short-term effects of a "health-at- every-size" approach on eating behaviors and appetite ratings. *Obesity* 2007;15:957 66.

320 Teixeira PJ, Silva MN, Coutinho SR, Palmeira AL, Mata J, Vieira PN, et al. Mediators of weight loss and weight loss maintenance in middle-aged women. *Obesity* 2009, 281.

321 Johnstone, AM. Fasting – the ultimate diet? *Obesity Reviews* 2007;8(3):211-222.

322 Clarke PB, Linzey, A. *Dictionary of ethics, theology and society.* Routledge Reference. Taylor & Francis. 1996;58.

323 Fatouros I, Chatzinikolaou A, Paltoglou G, et al. Acute resistance exercise results in catecholaminergic rather than hypothalamic–pituitary–adrenal axis stimulation during exercise in young men. *Stress: The International Journal on the Biology of Stress* 2010 Oct;13(6):461-468.

324 Mastorakos G et al. Exercise as stress model and the interplay between the hypothalamus-pituitary- adrenal and the hypothalamus-pituitary-thyroid axes *Horm Metab Res* 2005;37:577.

325 Kazushige Goto, Kohei Shioda, and Sunao Uchida. Effect of 2 days of intensive resistance training on appetite-related hormone and anabolic hormone responses. *Clin Physiol Funct Imaging* 2013;33:131–136.

326 Kuipers H. Training and overtraining: An introduction. *Med Sci Sports Exerc* 1998;30:1137–1139.

327 Jacoangeli F, Zoli A, Taranto A, et al, Osteoporosis and anorexia nervosa: Relative role of endocrine alterations and malnutrition. *Eat Weight Disord* 2002;7:190-195.

328 Phillips SM, Tipton KD, Aarsland A, Wolf SE, Wolfe RR. Mixed muscle protein synthesis and breakdown after resistance exercise in humans. *Am J Physiol Endocrinol Metab* 1997;273:E99–E107.

329 Dreyer HC, Fujita S, Cadenas JG, Chinkes DL, Volpi E, Rasmussen BB. Resistance exercise increases AMPK activity and reduces 4E-BP1 phosphorylation and protein synthesis in human skeletal muscle. *J Physiol* 2006;576:613–624.

330 Fujita S, Dreyer HC, Drummond MJ, Glynn EL, Volpi E, Rasmussen BB. Essential amino acid and carbohydrate ingestion prior to resistance

exercise does not enhance post-exercise muscle protein synthesis. J Appl Physiol. (1985)2009 May;106(5)1730-9.

331 Rennie MJ, Edwards RH, Halliday D, Matthews DE, Wolman SL, Millward DJ. Muscle protein synthesis measured by stable isotope techniques in man: The effects of feeding and fasting. *Clin Sci (Lond)* 1982;63:519–523.

332 Biolo G, Tipton KD, Klein S, Wolfe RR. An abundant supply of amino acids enhances the metabolic effect of exercise on muscle protein. *Am J Physiol Endocrinol Metab* 1997;273:E122–E129.

333 Kiens B, Roepstorff C, Glatz JF, Bonen A, Schjerling P, Knudsen J, and Nielsen JN. Lipid-binding proteins and lipoprotein lipase activity in human skeletal muscle: Influence of physical activity and gender. *J Appl Physiol* 2004; 97:1209–1218.

334 Epel ES. Psychological and metabolic stress: A recipe for accelerated cellular aging? *Hormones* 2009; 8(1):7-22.

335 Rutters F, Nieuwenhuizen AG, Lemmens SG, Born JM, Westerterp-Plantenga MS. Hyperactivity of the HPA axis is related to dietary restraint in normal weight women. *Physiol Behav* 2009;96:315-319.

336 Vigersky RA, Anderson AE, Thompson RH, and Loriaux DL. Hypothalamic dysfunction in secondary amenorrhea associated with simple weight loss. *N Engl J Med* 1977; 297:1141–1145.

337 Ursin H, Baade E, and Levine S. (Editors). *Psychobiology of Stress. A Study of Coping Men.* New York: Academic, 1978.

338 Mosek A, Korczyn AD. Fasting headache, weight loss, and dehydration. *Headache* 1999;29:225-227.

339 Dresher MJ, Elstein Y. Prophylactic COX 2 inhibitor: An end to the Yom Kippur headache. *Headache* 2006;26:1487-1491.

340 Soules MR, Merriggiola MC, Steiner RA, Clifton DK, Tiovala B, Bremmer WJ. Short-term fasting in normal women: Absence of effects on gonadotrophin secretion and the menstrual cycle. *Clin Endocrinol* 1994;40(6):725-31.

341 Olson BR, Cartledge T, Sebring N, Defensor R, Neiman L. Short-term fasting affects luteinizing hormone secretory dynamics but not reproductive function in normal-weight sedentary women. *J Clin Endocrinol Metab.* 1995;80(4):1187-93.

342 Alverno R, Kimzey L, Sebring N, Reynolds J, Loughran M, Nieman L, Olson BR. Effects of fasting of neuroendocrine function and follicle development in lean women. *J Clin Endocrinology and Metabolism* 1998; 83(1):76-80.

343 Mattson MP, Duan W, Guo Z. Meal size and frequency affect neuronal plasticity and vulnerability to disease: Cellular and molecular mechanisms. *Journal of Neurochemistry* 2003;84(3):417-431.

344 Bhasin S, Cryer PE, Vigersky R. *The Hormone Foundation's Patient Guide on the Diagnosis and Management of Hypoglycemic Disorders (Low Blood Sugar) in Adults.* The Hormone Foundation, 2009.

345 Alkén J, Petriczko E, Marcus C. Effect of fasting on young adults who have symptoms of hypoglycemia in the absence of frequent meals. *European Journal of Clinical Nutrition.* 2008 Jun;62(6):721-6.

346 Johnson JB, Summer W, Cutler RG et al. Alternate day calorie restriction improves clinical findings and reduces markers of oxidative stress and inflammation in overweight adults with moderate asthma. *Free Radical Biology & Medicine* 2007;42:665-674.

347 Aksungar FB, Topkaya AE, Akyildiz M. Interlukin-6, C-reactive protein and biochemical parameters during prolonged intermittent fasting. *Annals of Nutrition and Metabolism* 2007;51:88-95.

348 Martin B, Mattson MP, Maudsley S. Caloric restriction and intermittent fasting: Two potential diets for successful brain aging. *Aging Research Reviews* 2006;5:332-353.

349 Soules MR, Merriggiola MC, Steiner RA, Clifton DK, Toivola B, Bremner WJ. Short-Term fasting in normal women: absence of effects on gonadotrophin secretion and the menstrual cycle. *Clinical Endocrinology* 1994;40:725-731.

350 Funada J, Dennis AL, Roberts R, Karpe F, Frayn KN. Regulation of subcutaneous adipose tissue blood flow is related to measures of vascular and autonomic function. *Clinical Science.* 2010;119(8):313-322.

351 Trappe TA, White F, Lambert CP, Cesar D, Hellerstein M, Evans WJ. Effect of ibuprofen and acetaminophen on postexercise muscle protein synthesis. *American Journal of Physiology Endocrinology Metabolism.* 2002 Mar;282(3):E551-6.

352 Krentz JR, Quest B, Farthing JP, Quest DW, Chilibeck PD. The effects of ibuprofen on muscle hypertrophy, strength, and soreness during resistance training. *Applied Physiology Nutrition Metabolism.* 2008 Jun;33(3):470-5.

353 Hall MN. mTOR-what does it do? *Transplant Proc.* 2008;40:S5-8.

354 Glynn EL, Fry CS, Drummond MJ, Timmerman KL, Dhanani S, Volpi E, Rasmussen BB. Excess leucine intake enhances muscle anabolic signaling but not net protein anabolism in young men and women. *J Nutr.* 2010 Nov;140(11):1970-6.

355 Duffey KJ and Popkin BM. *Energy Density, Portion Size, and Eating Occasions: Contributions to Increased Energy Intake in the United States* 2011 Jun;8(6):e1001050.

356 Safdie FM, Dorff T, Quinn D, Fontana L, Wei M, et al. Fasting and cancer treatment in humans: A case report. *Aging.* 2009;1(12):1-20.